Is God Enough

for Such a Time as This

A Journey From the Darkness
of Homosexuality Into
the Light of God's Truth

Margaret Craig

ISBN 978-1-64492-645-1 (paperback)
ISBN 978-1-64492-646-8 (digital)

Christian Faith Publishing, Inc.
832 Park Avenue
Meadville, PA 16335
www.christianfaithpublishing.com

Printed in the United States of America

The Tribute

Andrae Crouch

To God the Father
Jesus Christ His Son
The Holy Spirit

How can I say thanks
For all the things you have done for me.
Things so underserved
Yet you gave to prove your love for me
And the voices of a million angels
Could not express my gratitude
All that I am and ever hope to be
I owe it all to Thee.

Just let me live my life
Let it be pleasing Lord, to Thee
Should I gain any praise
Let it go to Calvary.

With His blood He has saved me
With His power He has raised me
To God be the glory
For the things He has done.

MARGARET CRAIG

To God be the glory
To God be the glory
To God be the glory
For the things He has done.
With His blood He has saved me
With His power He has raised me
To God be the glory
For the things He has done.

Acknowledgments

I stand amazed as I look back and consider the people God has placed in my life to bring me where I am today.

I must begin with Jesse Sandberg. Thank you for your consistent love for me. Your encouragement, prompting, and wisdom have been very instrumental in getting this book written. I also need to thank Lois Stewart-Ferguson for the countless hours spent transferring my handwritten work onto the computer and basically being beside me from day one. We make a great team!

Thanks for my editor, Kimberly Barker, who has done a tremendous job, with much patience, in making sense of all I have written. Then to my friends who have stood beside me in prayer, always there with a listening ear and an encouraging word—Sandy, Ed and Sue, Barb, SOLOS, and my coworkers at the Flower Barn, to whom I am forever grateful. Thanks to all of you, and know I love and appreciate you deeply.

Introduction

For years, I have struggled with the idea of writing a book. It is an overwhelming task. Besides, who would even read it? Each time it was brought to mind, I would quickly dismiss the idea and move on to loving God and seeking His will for my life. I was quite sure writing a book was not part of His will—or so I thought. After all, I was very happy, free, content, and at total peace with God. I had a new life in Christ Jesus. Pleasing God and being obedient to Him and His Word are the deepest desires of my heart. Psalm 40:8 says, "I delight to do your will, O my God; your law is within my heart." In Isaiah 43:7, the Word of God tells us we were created for His glory.

Just how is it we glorify the creator of the universe? To me, it means to strive each day to love and obey Him with every breath and step I take; surrendering my will and seeking His to bring Him pleasure; to be salt and light to the world as Jesus commanded in the Sermon on the Mount (Matt. 5:3–16). We are also instructed to do as unto the Lord in all we do (Col. 3:23).

This past winter, a friend and her family spent Christmas in Florida while I remained in Michigan caring for their dog. When they left, we had very mild temperatures and not a snowflake in sight. Anyone who lives in Michigan knows the weather can and will change quickly. Sure enough, before they returned, temperatures dropped to near zero degrees with six to eight inches of fresh snow. I took their dog home before they arrived so he was there to greet them. The other thing greeting them was all that snow piled on their long driveway. Certain they didn't have boots with them, I decided to shovel a small path so they wouldn't get their feet wet. After the path was done, I decided to do just a little bit more.

I remember praying for their safe return and singing as I pushed the snow from side to side. Fortunately, it was very cold, so the snow was light and fluffy. It was perfect for shoveling but not so good for making snowmen. Before I knew it, I was finished! I remember smiling as I looked at the completely cleared driveway, and with joy in my heart, I said, "Thank you, Lord." I began the task with my friends in mind. Ultimately, it was for my Lord and His glory. What better way to communicate the love we hold in our hearts for God and His created people.

It's easy for me when obedience and serving means visiting someone in the hospital, mowing a neighbor's lawn, or taking home-made soup to a friend who is sick. Making cookies for a neighbor or surprising a friend on their birthday are all fun things, and I know they please my King. But obedience becomes much more difficult when we are called to speak the truth in love, stand firm, and confront a wrong.

As I sought God's will and direction in my life, He began to open doors. It was with much prayer, and great hesitation I might add, that I walked through those doors. I was given many opportunities to share my testimony at churches, women's conferences, and in Sunday school classes.

My heart still breaks for the many who, through tears and hopelessness, shared their concern for a son, daughter, friend, or loved one caught in the mysterious lifestyle of homosexuality. I can still see the pain and grief in their eyes as they would cling to me and whisper, "Thank you for telling the truth and for giving me hope that God can forgive and transform anyone's life, even that of the homosexual."

First Timothy 4:10 tells us, "For to this end we toil and strive, because we have our hope set on the living God, who is the Savior of all people, especially of those who believe." We need not look far to see what happens to a people and their nation when God is not enough. Abortion is no longer frowned upon, same-sex marriage is now the law of the land, and now non-gender is being seriously considered in many areas. How on earth did we get here? We have gone from a responsible, God-fearing people to a people of entitlement and rights. It's all about me and what I want. The trouble is this has carried over to God and His Word. No longer do we hold it as authoritative and true.

The almighty, sovereign God has given us His divine Word—His instruction and love letter to His children.

It is with conviction, tears, and great compassion that I write this book, stating what I know to be true based on the Word of God and His transforming work in my life.

Chapter 1
Many Roads to Happiness

In the beginning, God created the heavens and
the earth.

—Genesis 1:1

The older we get, the more the things that once seemed so important become less important. What didn't seem to matter before is now at the top of the list. I recently did a survey with friends asking the question: what is it that makes you happy? What is the American dream? Of course, the children wanted to become astronauts, hit a home run in the World Series with bases loaded, or become firefighter so they could ride the big red truck and blow the siren. Teens wanted to be left alone or maybe even become the next Elvis. People in their twenties, thirties, and even forties seemed to believe success was a career or a big home with a four-car garage and a Cadillac, truck, boat, and snowmobile to fill them.

My older friends seemed to think success is property up north for the summer and a condo in Florida to escape the brutal winters Michigan can deliver. I love it when my Christian brothers and sisters respond with the statement of obeying God. They believe, as I do, that obeying and pleasing God is the answer to a happy life. The term "peace and love" came up often, and I would add one more thing to that: "truth." If you can find these things somewhere in your life, you are on the right road.

It's a jungle out there! That is exactly the view I had of my life at this point in time as I walked in the park with my dog, Tolo. I began to wonder where and how it was that I got on this mysterious path

I seemed to be on. I was now thirty-six years old with a secure job. I had a home and enjoyed good health. I was not married, but I was living with someone who loved me very much. I've been living with this person for over six years and knew I was loved and enjoyed coming home to someone. So why is it that I was not on top of the world or, as some would put it, "had the tiger by the tail"? What is it that kept the quiet peace from me? Could it possibly be because the person I was living with was another woman? *So what?* I asked myself. We had a great relationship. We lived well together, traveled together, shared holidays, laughed and cried together, and had a great love and care for one another. I was loved and accepted, and that should cause me to feel complete. So why didn't I have any satisfying peace?

As a child, I struggled to be loved and accepted. I was the second of four children. My parents, being sure and hoping I was a boy, chose a male name before I was born. I was not only I a girl but also had a birth mark, which made me less than perfect in their eyes. Oh, don't get me wrong. My parents did their best raising me, caring for and loving me even though they were disappointed. For that, I am grateful. They had a form of religion but didn't attend church regularly. We went to church for weddings, funerals, and holidays—the times everyone attends to be socially accepted and please God.

But I was different, and I needed something different to get me through, especially in my childhood days. I was a marked child and different from all the other children. Being imperfect, I remember I would slap and bite my hand, hating my birthmark. I begged my mother to fix it, but she said, "There's nothing I can do, and you'll have to accept it." I was about four years old at the time. I didn't even know the meaning of the word *accept* let alone try to do it. This may not be a big deal to most people, but try going to school being different. Kids can be and are often cruel, and they lived up to every bit of that statement. I'm not going into detail, but I will say, it wasn't fun and I dreaded going to school every day.

However, I was fortunate to have loving grandparents who lived close by and loved me, looking beyond my imperfections. My desire was to be with them as much as I could because they showed love and care for me. They spoiled me as grandparents do, buying me things and letting me do what made me happy. What really made me happy was playing on the beach, going swimming with my sister Rachel. Those were the happy times. I remember my grandmother would buy me a doll, and my grandfather would buy me a truck. I chose to play with the truck. My grandmother would buy a teddy bear and my grandfather a football. I chose the football. Most people would try to analyze this, but don't—at this point.

You need to understand my grandfather was the apple of my eye. *Grandpa* was my first word. I would do anything and everything to please him. His favorite nickname for me was "Butch," which carried through all my life until my grandparents passed away. Their love and acceptance were very important to me as a child. Most would agree grandparents love you no matter what and enjoy spoiling you. My grandmother went to church every Sunday, and when I stayed with her, she made sure I went with her. As a child, I remember she always wore a medal of Jesus on a cross around her neck. One day, sitting on her lap, I asked the question of questions. "Grandma why is my hand red and none of the other kids have a red hand?"

She thought for what seemed to be eternity and spoke, "Butch, God picked you out of all the children and gave this special gift to you."

That made me feel pretty proud for about five minutes. I had to go back and face the kids every day at school, and God wasn't anywhere around to help me out—so I thought. My days consisted of looking for acceptance, only to find harsh words and rejection. My schoolmates held to their mean, old selves. The name-calling and rejection soon became part of my painful life. That famous old saying "Sticks and stones may break my bones, but names will never hurt me" is untrue and a lie of all lies. The names may not break any bones, but they break your heart. The special gift from God was far beyond my understanding or capability. I didn't see God coming to my rescue and punching those kids in my defense. After all, He was the one who made me with the birthmark.

Living next to a gracious, loving Christian family brought a sense of safety and connection. Their youngest child, Susan, was my age, and we were "buddies." She didn't care or even notice that

I had a red hand. She had an older brother who included us many times in the games of baseball, basketball, and football. I'm sure he just needed us to complete a team. Needless to say, we became very good at sports. I would find out that later in life, this would be an acceptable tool to be included as part of a team and, even later, give me a reason to want to be in school and even graduate. Susan and I remained friends all through high school. Her mother had a pleasing, kind, accepting demeanor about herself, often brushing my hair and making clothes for me and inviting me for lunch, dinner, and sleepovers. These were happy memories of my childhood, and I'm so grateful I was loved and accepted and lived next door to the Brooks family.

While in public grade school, we would say the Pledge of Allegiance and the Lord's Prayer at the beginning of each day. Next door to the school were retired missionaries who invited anyone who wanted to come during their recess or lunch hour to hear flannelgraph Bible stories. I heard the stories of Moses, Noah, and God's Son who loved me so much He died on the cross for my sins. I loved hearing those stories of love and didn't want to go back to school but rather remain there where I felt safe and accepted. I also got a hug every time I came in and left.

I attended Sunday school many times with Susan but also at the neighborhood church with my sister. The kids there were somewhat different from high school, but I still felt separate and different. I remember hearing the Bible stories again. I learned the Lord's Prayer, John 3:16, and Psalm chapter 23. These verses always seemed to bring a sense of belonging.

High school became more of a challenge as the rejection was much greater. While others were dating, going to dances, and proms, I was alone and unaccepted. Who would ask a girl with a red hand to a dance?

I survived and graduated *only* because I was chosen to be a part of sports activities, and I was good at them. On the ball field, it was my performance that mattered, not my appearance. Of course, an acceptable academic score was necessary to play on the varsity team. At one time, I was required to read two books prior to a game that was to be played in two days, and I did it! Why? Because I was an important part of the team—that's always a good feeling.

Susan went on to be married and asked me to be her maid of honor. I was thrilled to be a part of this happy occasion but wasn't comfortable with this future. While my classmates went on to college and marriage, I was stuck in the neighborhood playing ball with kids much younger than me. We had fun together because it didn't seem to matter to them that I was different. It made me feel special and wanted. I felt much peace and ease with them. Still there was an emptiness and void in my heart. I would go home after the game feeling alone and separated. The acceptance I found on the ball field no longer met my inner needs. I had a desire to love and be loved.

It was at this time a friend from high school named Sharon, whom I played sports with, started to show me special attention. I knew she was raised in a Christian family who attended church three times a week with parents who held strongly to Biblical guidelines. They were also strict and religious!

While I was babysitting for a neighborhood family, I invited Sharon to spend the weekend with me at their house. I was not prepared for what was about to happen. Because of our close friendship, she felt the liberty to show me affection in ways I was not familiar with—holding, hugging, and touching. I had no idea what was happening. I knew Sharon as a Christian. She was introduced to the holding, hugging, and touching by Kelli who was a pastor's daughter. In my mind, this must mean it's not only okay but also accepted.

I was unaware of these affections and where it would lead. Remember, this was 1960. The word *homosexuality* was not openly discussed. Confused as to what was going on, I felt loved but also had feelings of confusion and shame. My thoughts began to recall the stories I heard as a child of the God who sent His Son, Jesus, to die for my sins. I began asking, "Could this be okay? And if it is, why am I feeling ashamed and fearful that others will become aware of my actions?" At this point, I was sure I was the only one walking around with these feelings.

By this time, I began going to church to learn more about the God who loved me, the Jesus who died for my sins, and about heaven and hell. I didn't know much about these things other than there was a heaven and hell, and I believed God would decide where I'd spend eternity. Sharon and I began attending church together, and it felt good. Why wasn't there any peace? Where can it be found? Was I looking in the right place? If this was the right place, why didn't I want to tell others I had Sharon as my partner? Why did I feel the need to keep this a secret?

After a short time, Sharon left me for another woman. There I was again, abandoned, all by myself, lost, rejected, torn, and alone. Where do I go? I knew on the ball field with the young boys in the neighborhood, I would be accepted and loved. In fact, they waited anxiously for me to come. They were excited to see me, making me feel special and needed. It was where I truly fit!

Three boys who were always there lived across the street from the ball field. One hot afternoon, these boys invited me to their house for a cold drink. It was there I met their mother who didn't even notice my birthmark or that I was different. I wondered what she knew about me. Was I going to be accepted or rejected? Much to my surprise, I not only got my thirst quenched but also got accepted unconditionally. I spent much time at the Stewarts' home, feeling loved and like a part of their family. I began to watch these boys and their parents attend church, eat meals together, ride bikes, wash cars, mow lawns, and do many other activities. My desire was to be a part of "a family," and I was invited many times to share with them.

I remember like it was yesterday leaving their house wearing a cutoff sweatshirt and dirty jeans, just having fun playing ball, when their mom put her arms around me and said, "Margaret, I love you." I can honestly say it was at that time I felt loved by a family who included me. I was invited to live with them for a short period of time because of conflicts within my own household. I was invited to attend church with them on different occasions, and I did. The Bible was never preached at me but was open and apparent. I began seeing God's example displayed. Much of their life was to show kindness and love to one another (in fact, even to those who were not of their own family). This was just the beginning of a safe, open relationship. I was included in this love, and I fit.

Is God enough for such a time as this?

Chapter 2
Unchartered Waters

By this time in my life, most of my classmates were either married or in college pursuing their careers. Having graduated from high school by the skin of my teeth, going back to school was not an option for me. I wanted no part of that rejection again. Now I was in survival mode. The Stewart family was still a very important part of my life. Again, there, I felt loved and accepted. The deep desire to have someone special of my own was nagging at my inner being, so I pursued and was willing to learn about the lifestyle that could fulfill my desire to be loved. In doing so, I seemed to fit. At this time, I was living with someone who welcomed me home after a long day at work. It felt good and right. Yes, it was another woman, but so what?

My mind returned to the Bible stories told on the flannelgraph, the Sunday school class, and songs like "Jesus Loves Me" and "This Little Light of Mine." These were words that would not leave me alone. I didn't feel like Jesus loved me at all, and if so, something was missing. That something was peace. As far as "This Little Light of Mine," to tell you the truth, all I saw was darkness. I didn't want to do anything that separated me from the God I learned about as a child. Now the search began. Where do I go to find truth? Who do I talk to? Who will understand? How do I know who to trust? When I hear the truth, will I understand it to be truth? All these questions kept racing through my mind. Now I sought out this new type of love I didn't quite understand. I did feel loved, wanted, and needed. It was something I was searching for as a child and now as an adult. It can't be wrong because it felt so right. I didn't want to give up the acceptance and love now that I had found it. But again, the question was why was there no peace in this newfound love? While searching, I looked in all the seemingly right places: the bowling alley, the ball field, the gay bars, and yes, even the gay churches. After all, I felt the need to include God in my life. Up until now, I had three different unbelieving partners. Maybe what I really needed was a Christian partner—one who believed in God.

In the gay community, God is always discussed very openly, and many practicing homosexuals feel sure they are safe and accepted in His love although this is never absolute. They seem to have all the answers. The scriptures dealing with this lifestyle are just man's interpretation. Another example: God created Eve for only Adam's helpmate, not necessarily every other male form. Being a homosexual is no different than being left-handed. I had it justified, but there were still unanswered questions within. It wasn't being a lesbian that brought unhappiness, unrest, and misery to my heart and soul. It was the inability to line up my lifestyle with God and His Word.

Finally, I found that Christian partner. Lori came from a Christian home, attended church regularly, and seemed to know the old familiar Bible stories I knew. Together, we attended the gay church, which I was happy about, but I began to see the drastic difference between the church we were attending and the church I attended with the Stewart family. I remember sitting in the gay church with Lori and feeling so out of place (not belonging). I was afraid the God I had heard about as a child was different from the God this church believed in. I remember reading a poem written by Jessie Rice Sandberg, whom you will hear more about later in this book, which seemed to speak to my heart. The poem entitled "I Am Waiting, Lord" by Jessie Rice Sandberg seemed to meet my fears.

> I am waiting, Lord, and I feel immobilized by fear
> frozen by the things I do not understand.
> I cannot step ahead toward goals
> that once seemed so attainable.
>
> Late storms have brought disaster to my landscape.
> Familiar things seem somehow not to sit quite soundly
> on their old foundations.

IS GOD ENOUGH FOR SUCH A TIME AS THIS

Strange shifts of angles in the shape of forms
once stable and secure confuse me,
make me lose my compass point.

Where to turn? What to do?

I have no clue as to the future.
My options have dissolved and trickled away
with the run-off from the storm.

And so I wait

Lord, help me not to simply sit among my broken things,
turning them over and over in my hands,
grieving for the past.
Teach me in my waiting to find the valued remnants
and store them in a place quiet and safe.

Help me to take the time
to bury dead dreams with dignity
not to wallow in regrets
nor to collect small grievances.

Let nothing be wasted in this crisis that has seemed
to stop the clock and lock the door
to all I felt most precious.

Help me to watch beyond my altered skyline
for that first faint glow of morning sun.
Let me wrap myself in faith
and snuggle down with hope.

Help me to discern, even now,
the soft gilding of these ruins with early dawn.
Let me see, approaching with the morning light,
the form of Him
Who stills the storm and transforms with His presence.

At this point, it seemed every time I tried to get closer to God, I found myself more confused and separated. I was beginning to feel an urgent fear of God because I knew He was not only the creator of all things but also sovereign and judge.

Lori began to see the uneasiness within me. The more confused and fearful I became, the more I ran back to the place I felt safe and loved—to Lois Stewart, who always made time and showed love just for me! Because of this, I was unwilling to share my involvement with Lori for fear of rejection. Still I felt drawn and never wanted to leave that place of refuge. The gay lifestyle is jealous, empty, and selfish. Because of this, Lori resented Lois Stewart and the times I wanted to run in her direction. It was always taking time away from her. She felt she was losing me, and she was. Her plan was to destroy the relationship I had with Lois and the family. Desperate and hoping she could destroy any bonds, she went to Lois's office and exposed our lifestyle. Up until that point, I had questioned whether Lois knew of our relationship. I did my best to keep it private. I always feared the day it would be exposed and the consequences. Lori met me at the door when I returned home from work and explained what she had done. I knew what was coming: I was going to be rejected and lose the relationship I so cherished. Lori then told me, "Lois wants to see you tonight."

I said out loud, "I'm sure she does."

I only lived a mile from their house, but it took forty-five minutes to get there as I was afraid of the words I anticipated. I arrived while they were eating dinner, and naturally, Lois grabbed her Bible and we left together in her car. This wasn't something we would discuss around the dinner table with members of the family present. I remember the silence that seemed like forever while the Bible sat between us.

Lois pulled into a parking lot while speaking. "You know I can't condone the lifestyle you are living with Lori." At the time, she picked up the Bible, demonstrating her stand and belief that God's Word would not accept homosexuality but rather condemn it as sin. Her next words were most comforting: "Whatever you choose, I will always love you."

She asked if I wanted to accept Christ as my Savior, and my immediate answer was no. It was not that I was rejecting Christ, but I was confused and unsure if Christ could really forgive me and if I could change.

Returning home, I remember getting out the car and Lois asking, "Do you remember what I said?"

I said yes, mumbling under my breath, "You couldn't condone my lifestyle."

Again, Lois reminded me she would always love me no matter what I chose. I trusted and knew Lois would always be loving and accepting of me. This trust was built through several years of me running away and then returning to find acceptance from Lois and her family. I had someone on my side—finally!

Upon arriving back home, I found Lori anxiously waiting for me, feeling sure my relationship with Lois and the Stewart family was finished. The rest of the evening was very silent as I went into my room and closed the door. I was going over and over the conversation Lois and I had in the car. Now my heart was divided because God wanted no part of my lifestyle. I began to see why there was no peace. Lori knew she was losing me. Even though we continued to attend the gay church, I was unable to sit there and listen, so we would get up and leave. I would return to church with Lois and the Stewart family. I couldn't sit there either, but I always ran back to Lois. I was drawn because of the unconditional love that had been offered and displayed. Not ready to let go, Lori came with me several times as I visited and talked with Lois. I began to see the different types of love displayed. Lori's love, on one hand, was very conditional and demanding. Lois, on the other hand, displayed freedom and unconditional love, demonstrating the way Christ loves His children.

Is God enough for such a time as this?

Chapter 3
The Path to Truth

You will seek me and find me, when you seek me
with all your heart.

—Jeremiah 29:13

Lori and I had, on occasion, visited Lois as she always accepted us
even though we were still together in a relationship. I was sure Lois
knew she and I believed differently. On one particular day, Lori and
I walked through Lois's door unannounced, as Lori was not willing
to give up on our relationship. I have no idea where Lori's thoughts
were, but I knew she wasn't ready to surrender our relationship for
something she didn't believe. I knew I was still trying to find the
place where God would fit into our relationship. After all, we loved
each other.

After casual conversation, Lois invited us to read with her from
the Bible. We each had a different translation while Lois read Romans
1:16–32.

> For I am not ashamed of the gospel, for it is the
> power of God for salvation to everyone who
> believes, to the Jew first and also to the Greek.
> For in it the righteousness of God is revealed
> from faith for faith, as it is written, "The righ-
> teous shall live by faith."
>
> For the wrath of God is revealed from
> heaven against all ungodliness and unrighteous-
> ness of men, who by their unrighteousness sup-

press the truth. For what can be known about God is plain to them, because God has shown it to them. For his invisible attributes, namely, his eternal power and divine nature, have been clearly perceived, ever since the creation of the world, in the things that have been made. So they are without excuse. For although they knew God, they did not honor him as God or give thanks to him, but they became futile in their thinking, and their foolish hearts were darkened. Claiming to be wise, they became fools, and exchanged the glory of the immortal God for images resembling mortal man and birds and animals and creeping things.

Therefore God gave them up in the lusts of their hearts to impurity, to the dishonoring of their bodies among themselves, because they exchanged the truth about God for a lie and worshiped and served the creature rather than the Creator, who is blessed forever! Amen.

For this reason God gave them up to dishonorable passions. For their women exchanged natural relations for those that are contrary to nature; and the men likewise gave up natural relations with women and were consumed with passion for one another, men committing shameless acts with men and receiving in themselves the due penalty for their error.

And since they did not see fit to acknowledge God, God gave them up to a debased mind to do what ought not to be done. They were filled with all manner of unrighteousness, evil, covetousness, malice. They are full of envy, murder, strife, deceit, maliciousness. They are gossips, slanderers, haters of God, insolent, haughty, boastful, inventors of evil, disobedient to parents, foolish, faithless, heartless, ruthless. Though they know God's righteous decree that those who practice such things deserve to die, they not only do them but give approval to those who practice them.

As Lois read the words, I intently followed along. Two things from the passage of Romans chapter 1 seemed to pierce my mind and heart. First, it states all men have the knowledge of God and are without excuse. Second, the phrase "God gave them over" caused me to question whether God would abandon me or not. As I raised my head from the pages in front of me, I saw a divided room. Good and evil. Righteousness and unrighteousness. Heaven and hell. The words "God gave them over" kept ringing in my ears, and a deep, deep sense of separation came over me and seemed to possess my whole being. Have you ever been in such a state that you couldn't speak? I was not only speechless but also couldn't even move. Something had a grip on my very soul that I still have trouble describing. I didn't know whether to sit still or run.

Lori immediately stood to leave, taking me with her. The Stewart home was my home and always a safe refuge for me. I sure didn't want to leave then but soon found myself in the car on my way home. Lois hugged me as I left, reassuring me of her promise: "No matter what you choose, I will always love you." It was then the shades of darkness were removed from my eyes and the blanket of deceit torn from my heart. Bottom line, the lifestyle I was living was sin and an abomination toward God, and I was separated from Him. Wow! Did I sleep that night? *Absolutely not*. I wasn't sure I wanted to be in the same house with Lori, let alone the bedroom, nor was I willing to change from my clothes to my pajamas. Fear overcame me as I knew there was a huge battle before me. Was I strong enough, smart enough, or even courageous enough to survive? What I didn't know at the time was it was God doing the fighting for my soul.

The next morning, I remember it being my day off. I wanted to run to Lois and talk about what I had heard the evening before that kept piercing my heart and causing me to sleep restlessly. Lori insisted on going with me as she was not ready to let go. She was still hanging on to every part of me. I remember walking in the door—I never had to knock because I was always welcome and part of the family. This was way before cell phones, so I usually appeared unannounced. As always, Lois stopped what she was doing and made time for me. During our conversation, Lois looked at Lori and asked the question, "Do you love Margaret?"

Lori responded quickly and forcefully, "Yes, of course I do. I would do anything for her."

Lois's next words were, "Do you love her enough to move out of her bedroom?"

Lori's defiant answer was, "No, I will not."

I remember being surprised at the sharp contrast in her answer. The love Lois displayed was faithful and unconditional. The love Lori displayed was very conditional, and I was expected to meet her needs. Again, a division was brought to light. I told Lois I wanted to purchase a Bible of my own and asked her what I should buy. She wrote on a piece of paper what I should buy, and I was off to the Bible bookstore with Lori tagging along. I found the Bible I wanted to purchase and was ready to leave, but Lori was looking at different translations. I asked her what she was doing, and she answered with these all-telling words: "I'm trying to find where it says it differently." Evidently, she heard the words I had heard: "God gave them over." I remember we stayed in the store for over an hour looking for something she was unable to find.

The days ahead seemed like an eternity, still searching and seeking peace while Lori remained living in the house. There seemed to be a storm raging inside me. What I did notice was the path was lighter now as the light seemed to overpower darkness. Glimmers of hope seemed to appear everywhere I turned. The darkness that once engulfed my mind, heart, and soul now seemed to be fading. My mind could clearly see the answer I had been searching for: truth. However, this was not the answer I anticipated. I had done my research by attending a gay church and seeking counsel with Lori. I attended a local church and talked with the pastor. Mind you, it was not a gay church. After an hour of spilling my struggles and stating

I had no peace while living with Lori (living in the homosexual life-style), he gently put his hand on my shoulder and said my problem was with commitment. God made me to be gay, and I needed to stop fighting this fact, accept it, and move on. There it was. I had my affirmation and stamp of approval from the church. A pastor and representative of the Word of God said, "It's okay."

Maybe a part of me was still holding on to any hope that living in the lesbian lifestyle was okay. It seemed I had all the approval and support I would need. I found myself only more confused and with-out peace. I stayed awake most of the night trying to process in my mind what was taking place. Since I had my own Bible, I read and reread Romans chapter 1. The words seemed to jump off the page into my very being: "They exchanged the truth for a lie, and God gave them over to a depraved mind." Yet a pastor, whom one would think could be trusted, affirmed that God made me this way. Looking back, I believe Jeremiah 29:13 took a solid stand in my life: "You will seek me and find me, when you seek me with all of your heart."

Is God enough for such a time as this?

Chapter 4
Finding My Way to Christ

If you confess with your mouth that Jesus is Lord
and believe in your heart that God raised him
from the dead, you will be saved. For with the
heart one believes and is justified, and with the
mouth one confesses and is saved.

—Romans 10:9–10

I would continue showing up at church where Lois and her family
attended. There was a definite difference between the gay church
and this body of believers. One Sunday evening, in 1985, I remember attending service. I always sat in the back row in case I needed
to make a quick exit as I did many times before. I remember it like
it was yesterday. Lois, along with two other women (Delphine and
Star), sang the special music that night. It was the music God chose
knowing I was ready to surrender my heart to Him. The name of the
song is "Someone is Praying for You" by Don Moen. These are the
words I heard:

Someone is praying for you
Have the clouds round you gathered
in the midst of a storm.
Is your ship tossed and battered,
Are you weary and worn.
Don't lose hope someone is praying for you this very day
And peace be still is already on the way.

When it seems that you've prayed till your strength is all gone
And your tears fall like raindrops all the day long
He is there and He knows just how much you can bear
He'll speak your name to someone in prayer

Someone is praying for you
Someone is praying for you
So when it seems you are all alone
and your heart would break in two
remember someone is praying for you.

At the conclusion of the service, I waited for Lois—the one person I trusted. In tears, I told her I wanted to pray. She said, "Do you want to go to the altar and pray?"

"No," I replied. I didn't feel I was good enough. "Can't we just go home?"

We went to her home, and it was there, on my knees, I confessed I was a sinner and asked Christ into my life. Did I believe He heard me and came into my heart? Yes. Did I believe He could not only forgive me but also give me a clean heart? No. I only knew it was where I needed to start. Instead of joy filling my heart at that moment, I was consumed with uncertainty and loneliness. It was obvious I couldn't continue in the lifestyle I had been living for twenty years.

Fear filled me as I drove home to face Lori. She was still hanging on to any part of me she could. She greeted me as I walked into the house with her usual hug. While she embraced me, I felt a cold chill running all through my body. As she held on, I froze. For a few seconds, it seemed as though evil itself had its arms wrapped around me. Suddenly, Lori pushed herself away from me as if in shock. I then told her I had prayed and asked Christ into my life and went to a separate bedroom. I didn't come out until the next morning when I knew Lori had left for work. At the first moment I could, I ran back to Lois. She was at work, but that didn't stop me nor did it seem to upset her. I'm sure she knew I was stressed. I remember blurting out, "I need Lori to move out of my house. I can't live with that constant reminder of my past, not to mention the temptation."

I don't like to hurt people and knew it would be difficult to ask her to leave. Lois hugged me, and we prayed. She reassured me everything would be okay and said, "God is in control."

To me, those were just words. Deep down inside, I knew God wasn't going to listen to me, but maybe—just maybe—He would listen to Lois. I headed home, all the while trying to find the right words to make Lori understand. I couldn't live with her any longer, and I had no desire to live with her. Ready for battle, I pulled into the driveway and walked into the house to find an unexpected release. Not only was she not there; she had also taken all her personal belongings—everything including the toothbrush in the bathroom. Not a trace of her was left. Coincidence? Not at all, knowing what I know now: "For when I am weak, then I am strong" (2 Cor. 12:10b).

After twenty years of living in that lifestyle, I walked away from the gay bars, the gay church, gay softball league, and the community, breaking all ties. I walked away from that world into an unknown community: God's people and His church.

Is God enough for such a time as this?

Chapter 5
Transformation of the Heart

> Therefore, if anyone is in Christ, he is a new creation. The old has passed away; behold, the new has come.
> —2 Corinthians 5:17

Walking away from a lifestyle of twenty years was going to be a difficult task. Other than work and family, my time was spent in the gay community where most of my friends were. Needless to say, I now had a sense of emptiness and loneliness—a big hole in my life. The interesting point here is I no longer wanted to be a part of that community, yet I was very uncertain of the path that lay ahead. Something incredible had transpired within me. My desires and emotions had changed. How is it that I was able be comfortable most of my life in a lifestyle with someone who loved me and whom I loved back? Now, all of a sudden, that comfort has been removed. Conviction, shame, and guilt took its place. When that happened, the only thing I knew to do was confess it to Christ and turn from it. I believe the correct word for that would be *repent*. I had totally surrendered all I was and all I had done to Christ who is faithful to forgive and cleanse us from all unrighteousness.

The Gospel of John speaks of a blind man Jesus had healed. There are several important aspects of this story, but there is one that stuck in my mind. The Pharisees who had been trying to trap and discredit Jesus had asked the blind man how he had received his sight. The man responded, "He put mud on my eyes. I washed them, and now I see."

This all took place on the Sabbath, which was another strike against Jesus according to the righteous Pharisees. Again, the Pharisees asked the man, "How did Jesus open your eyes?"

What did He do? The blind man replied, "All I know is once I was blind, and now I see."

That's the best way I can explain the instant change within me. Not only did Christ create in me a new heart and spirit but also gave me a sense of peace I was searching and longing for all my life—a peace that passes all understanding (Phil. 4:7). It only makes sense that to obtain that deep peace, one must be at peace with God.

A new heart and a changed life began—a mystery, for sure. Remember Nicodemus who was a Pharisee and ruler of the Jews? He had heard Jesus teaching on many occasions and witnessed several miracles He had performed. Jesus had caused the blind to see, the lame to walk, and had even raised Lazarus from the dead. How can one be a witness to these miracles and not be the least bit curious? John 3:1–2 tells us Nicodemus did acknowledge Jesus as a teacher come from God, for no one can do these signs. It is with this visit from Nicodemus that Jesus made this astounding statement: "Truly, truly, I say to you, unless one is born again he cannot see the kingdom of God" (John 3:3).

Perplexed by this (and who wouldn't be?), Nicodemus naturally responds with, "How can a man be born when he is old? Can he enter a second time into this mother's womb and be born?"

Jesus answered, "Truly, truly, I say to you, unless one is born of water and the Spirit, he cannot enter into the kingdom of God. That which is born of the flesh is flesh, and that which is born of the Spirit is spirit" (John 3:4–6.)

Regeneration, or being born again, is immediate and an act of God alone. It is only by His love and grace that we are spiritually made alive. We were once spiritually dead. It is also here, when Jesus is talking with Nicodemus, that He quoted the famous verse we all know and have memorized: "For God so loved the world, that he gave his only Son, that whoever believes in him should not perish but have eternal life" (John 3:16).

To make this personal, God so loved Margaret that He sent His Son to die on the cross for my sins so that I might have eternal life with God. I like to personalize God's Word as if He had me in mind when He spoke it. When one thinks about it, God did have us in mind—you and me. So with that, I read this verse: "God so loved Margaret that He gave His only Son, that if Margaret believes in Him she should not perish but have eternal life."

Wow! How does one even grasp that kind of love from the almighty God, the creator and maker of all things? I lack the words that even begin to describe His love for me. I believe the hymn writer Federick M. Lehman penned it best in the song "The Love of God."

The love of God is greater far
Than tongue or pen can ever tell;
It goes beyond the highest star,
And reaches to the lowest hell;
The guilty pair, bowed with care,
God gave His Son to win:
His erring child He reconciled,
And pardoned from his sin.

When years of time shall pass away,
And earthly thrones and kingdoms fall,
When men, who here refuse to pray,
On rocks and hills and mountains call,
God's love so sure shall still endure,
All measureless and strong;
Redeeming grace to Adam's race—
The saints' and angels' song.

Could we with ink the ocean fill,
And were the skies of parchment made,
Were every stalk on earth a quill,
And every man a scribe by trade;
To write the love of God above
Would drain the ocean dry;

Nor could the scroll contain the whole,
Though stretch from sky to sky.

Refrain:
O love of God, how rich and pure!
How measureless and strong!
It shall forevermore endure—
The saints and angels song.

The only honest to goodness way to experience this kind of love is to be reconciled to God. God sent His Son, Jesus, to pay the penalty of our sins so we can be reconciled to Him. Because of sin, we have been separated from God. Upon receiving Jesus Christ, we, therefore, have been reconciled to Him because He settled the dispute through His blood on the cross for all men who would come to Him confessing sin and believing. It is our responsibility to take hold of that truth by confessing our sin, repenting, and, in faith, believing in Christ alone. The result is being born again, as I mentioned earlier.

Regeneration is the gift of God's grace and is vital in the life of a new believer, mainly because it is required even to enter God's kingdom. It is nothing of ourselves or anything we do. No part of us is even involved. It is an act of God alone. "Create in me a clean heart, O God, and renew a right spirit within me" (Ps. 51:10). Another version states, "Create in me a clean heart, O God. Renew a loyal spirit within me" (NLT).

This new heart is now filled with the desire to do God's will, not my own. A desire to know Him more, to love Him, worship Him, and obey Him, thus to bring glory and honor to His name. Upon receiving this new heart when we are born again, the Holy Spirit lives within us, never to leave us to ourselves. This power of the Holy Spirit enables us to live a changed lifestyle. I believe the main purpose of the Holy Spirit is to glorify Jesus Christ, God's Son, by working in believers to the will and work of God.

Is God enough for such a time as this?

Chapter 6
A New Identity

I have been crucified with Christ. It is no longer
I who live, but Christ who lives in me. And the
life I now live in the flesh I live by faith in the Son
of God, who loved me and gave himself for me.
                                        —Galatians 2:20

For the first time in my life, I felt alive and free. Returning to work, several of my friends noticed something different about me. Tina had even asked, "What happened to you? You're glowing and seem different." Today, if that were asked of me, I'd be ready and willing to share the reason for the joy and hope within me.

"But in your hearts honor Christ the Lord as holy, always being prepared to make a defense to anyone who asks you for a reason for the hope that is in you; yet do it with gentleness and respect" (1 Pet. 3:15). I wasn't ready nor did I even know how to explain what had taken place. I was a brand-new believer—a baby Christian. It would be like taking a newborn baby to the woods and leaving it there to survive on its own.

I began attending Five Points Community Church where I had gone on occasion with the Stewart family. I felt accepted and welcomed. I am sure it was mostly because of Lois who invited me week after week. I was confident I would be accepted, and I knew I would be accepted because of her faith and testimony within the church. It was only because of that witness I was able to walk through the doors. I stuck to her side like superglue.

Remember, this was back in the eighties, when you didn't see women wearing slacks in church. I came as I was—jeans, black leather boots, and my wallet in my hip pocket with a chain hanging from it. I am sure this was quite a shock to the men in their suits and women in fine dresses and spiky heels. I was very different indeed! I was different, and I knew it. I can't imagine what went through the minds of the people, but God protected me from any form of separation or rejection. I knew all about rejection, and had I sensed it. I would have run in the opposite direction, never looking back. It was God's grace, mercy, and love that sustained me.

What I soon noticed was the desire to change my outward appearance. My heart and soul were now different and in no way corresponded with the way I dressed. So Lois and I went shopping together. I had no idea where to even start. I didn't have to look for clothes because my job required a uniform. Shopping is not one of my favorite things to do. The change was gradual, going from jeans and boots to skirts and low heels. I remember having to learn to walk all over again. Then it was time to buy a purse.

"I don't need a purse," I stated.

"Where do you keep all your stuff?" Lois asked.

"In my pockets," I answered.

Eventually, we did purchase a purse, but even today, I still carry my money in my back pocket. Some habits are difficult to change.

While attending church, I wanted to become involved in different areas of serving. I took a membership class, was baptized, and joined the church. I wanted to be baptized. It signifies the unity with Christ and His death, burial, and resurrection. Because I had accepted Jesus Christ as my personal savior, God freely gave me a new life, and I wanted to be identified with Him. He had sealed it with the abiding presence of the Holy Spirit who now lives within me. I am now safe in Christ forever. Amen!

The very first thing I wanted to do was join the women's softball team. I knew, there, I would be accepted and fit right in. After all, I grew up playing block baseball and could throw and hit with the best of them.

I also joined the choir because I love to sing. I remember how gracious the choir director, Lynn, was. I told her I couldn't read music, but I could follow someone. She placed me next to a strong alto, and we got along fine. The only problem I had was when I somehow got placed between a very strong alto and an extremely strong soprano. That Sunday, I sang a little bit of both. I have a dear friend, Jeannine, who always tells me when it comes to singing, "there are canaries and crows, and God loves them both the same." I am definitely a crow. After all, the Bible does say, "Make a joyful noise to the Lord." By the time my flat and off-key notes reach God in heaven, He would be hearing a clear and beautiful voice, like a Julie Andrews or a Sandi Patty. Now that is a true miracle and would take an act of God!

There was a total change inside me. The world that was comfortable to me before now seemed strange, dark, and very uneasy. I had attended the gay church and gay bars and many of my friends were gay, but that all changed. I had been part of a bowling league that primarily consisted of gay members. I did continue bowling with them as I had made a commitment with the team. However, I didn't seem to belong with this crowd any longer. "The eyes of my heart were enlightened..." (Eph. 1:18).

My desires, my dress, my friends, and my identity had changed. I was now a child of the King, wanting to please Him in all aspects. He was and is now Lord of my life!

I was enjoying my new life and serving the Lord. I enjoyed working with the teens and became a teen sponsor. It was all going well and then it happened—the teens were going away to winter camp for the weekend, and I was asked to go along. Up until then, no one had known anything about my past, and I was very content and guarded in keeping it that way. Before leaving for camp, Lois strongly suggested I share my past with the youth pastor, Dave Somers. It was only fair for him to know as he was accountable and responsible for the teens. I knew she was right, although that didn't make it any easier. I decided to wait until we got to camp. I am sure it was the Holy Spirit that guided me in making that decision. It was a four-hour bus ride north, and I used all that time searching for the right words.

I had a great respect for Pastor Dave as I watched him work with the teens. He was a godly man, kind, compassionate, and a wonderful teacher of God's Word. I told him I needed to talk with him, and we went for a walk in the woods. I then told him about my past and how God forgave me of my sins and delivered me from a homosexual lifestyle. He didn't blink twice, gasp, or even pause. He immediately put his arm around me and said, "Welcome to the family, and I'm so glad you are here." Wow! It didn't matter where I had been or what I had done. What did matter was I was now part of the family of sinners saved by grace. That, my friend, is a true example of the love of Christ— accepting and welcoming a believer into the community, Christ's church, a place to belong and serve among other believers.

The badge of a true Christian is love. It has to be in order to obey the two great commandments.

> And he said to him, "You shall love the Lord your God with all your heart and with all your soul and with all your mind. This is the great and first commandment. And a second is like it: You shall love your neighbor as yourself. On these two commandments depend all the Law and the Prophets." (Matt. 22:37–40)

Is God enough for such a time as this?

Chapter 7
Following Christ in Obedience

Therefore, my beloved, as you have always
obeyed, so now, not only as in my presence but
much more in my absence, work out your own
salvation with fear and trembling, for it is God
who works in you, both to will and to work for
his good pleasure.

—Philippians 2:12–13

Several years ago, I had a Doberman who had puppies. Everyone
came to see the six little Dobermans. Watching as they tumbled and
played with each other brought joy to many, being able to hold them
and to smell that puppy breath known to all who have experienced
an eight-week-old puppy in their life. My friend Karen wanted to
come visit and bring her two year old son, Adam, to play with the
puppies.

When Karen arrived, Adam was sound asleep in his car seat.
What happened next was an example and a good lesson from a two-
year-old that, to this day, is embedded in my mind.

"Wake up, Adam. We're here," said Karen.

"Okay, Mom," little Adam replied, rubbing his eyes with his
tiny hands.

"Say hi to Maggie."

"Okay, Mom. Hi, Maggie," he said with his little eyes only half
open.

Karen then reached in to help Adam from the back seat, saying,
"Come on. Let's get out."

"Okay, Mom," he responded quickly.

As we approached the puppies, you could see the eagerness in little Adam's face, wanting to touch and play with them.

"Adam, be nice. They are only babies."

"Okay, Mom," he said again.

His reward was sitting on the floor with two six-week-old puppies wagging their tails and crawling all over him. He was laughing and grinning from ear to ear. What impressed me most was his instant response and complete obedience to his mom's requests—"Okay, mom!" Seeing this example gave me a desire to have that same instant obedience and trust in God's requirements of me. I had a desire in my heart to know more about this God who created all things and also about His Son, Jesus, who died that I might have eternal life.

I joined Bible study and also began reading Scripture on my own. I remember reading John 14:15: "If you love me you will keep my commandments." I had given my all to Christ and loved Him with all my heart. My prayer daily was to serve Him and seek His will in order to please and glorify Him. I was happy doing that in different ministries of the church.

When I became a Christian, Jesus became Lord of my life. First Corinthians 6:19–20 says, "Or do you not know that your body is a temple of the Holy Spirit within you, whom you have from God? You are not your own, for you were bought with a price. So glorify God in your body." Christ now lives inside me! Again, it was no longer my will, but I had totally surrendered to His will. In order for that to happen, changes had to take place. I was not willing to give some things up, and it was painful when God removed them from me.

I had a boat and motor that was my grandfather's. I loved to go fishing and just be out on the water. I also had a four-wheel drive with which I pulled my boat. In the past, I would often hook my boat up and head up north. I loved my boat and truck maybe too much. I lost them both on the same day heading back from up north. My boat ended up down a hill and in the woods. An hour later, the engine of my truck blew. I was forty-five minutes from home on I-75 with Mendy, my Doberman, in the back seat. This was way before cell phones, and the next exit was about two miles down the road. Mendy and I had just started to walk toward the exit when a tow truck driver on the opposite side of the interstate turned his flashing lights on and came to my rescue. He said he was heading home from work and noticed I needed help. The kind man hooked my truck, put Mendy and me in the front seat, and delivered us safely home. I don't know if angels drive tow trucks, wear bib overalls, or smoke cigars, but he certainly was an angel coming to my rescue in my life at a much needed time. Oh, and my boat! Someone at church was looking for a boat and offered to go and get it. "It's all yours," I responded.

There were and are other things in my life I've had to let go, but I've come to know it's for my good. God not only knows but also wants what's best for me. My friend Jessie Rice Sandberg wrote an article I'd like to share with you. It's titled "The Day of the Great Takeover."

Hello!

You probably don't know me, I hardly know myself…

You see, I was one of the disaster victims… life absolutely shattered. I thought I was living well. I had let someone exciting pretty much take over my life. I had built this world—this house— around me—that was just for me! Parties every night… Doin' my own thing. Lots of adventure…burning the candle at both ends, I can't say it wasn't fun. After all I wasn't having to worry about anybody else's happiness but my own so I used people…cheated here and there…lived for the moment, the experience…did whatever felt good at the time…

But after a while it seemed to take more of everything to satisfy. I was running out of resources and the people in my life got tired of my using them. Besides...down deep inside there was this sick feeling. OK, I'll call it what it was—just plain old guilt. The truth is, I didn't like the looks of the house I had created—filth in every corner, lurid pictures everywhere and the smell—oh my, the smell. My house had become practically a garbage dump.

Finally, I crashed. Everything valuable to me was slipping away. I was at the end of my rope. Eventually someone told me that there was a rescue center nearby—a place where people could come just as they were.

I met a Person there who had the kindest eyes and the most welcoming smile I had ever seen. He was everything I had ever wanted to be. Suddenly I looked at myself and saw—for the first time—the person I really was.

I could tell by His eyes that He saw straight through me and knew everything about me.

"I am so ashamed," I said, as He reached out to take my hand. "I am a mess. I don't even know what to do with myself."

"Then I have good news for you." And He wrapped His arms around me.

He took me in and cleaned me up. Then He told me that I had been assigned a Mentor, a Resource Manager, a Personal Friend—a Person who would teach me what I needed to know and help me live the way I knew I needed to live. I can't tell you how glad I was to know that there was Someone Who would be looking out for me. Of course I knew I would have to clean up my act before He would want to hang around me. But I was certainly going to make Him proud! I was going to be the "poster child" of change.

I immediately decided that I would work as hard being the "good guy" as I had worked at having fun. I decided to separate from my old friends and hang out with the "nice" people— you know, the ones who do everything right. Everybody noticed this big change in me. I spent hours down at the Rescue Center doing anything that needed to be done. The people there keep me busy day and night. (I think they were trying to keep me out of trouble!)

I moved all the nasty stuff out of my house and did a major overhaul. Painted the walls and put up signs...nicely lettered you know... to remind myself of how I had to behave. I had the Ten Commandments in every room even though I had already memorized them. And I had all kinds of nice plaques: "A good deed every day," "Help the poor," "Be a good neighbor," you know the sort of thing.

It was a funny thing though: the more rules I made and the more I tried to keep them the more I could see of this nasty stuff building up that I had tried to get rid of. The rotten smell wasn't just coming from my house; it was coming from somewhere deeper inside me. I obviously still had a basic serious flaw. But I couldn't seem to fix it. I was getting irritable and tired and frustrated trying to keep things clean...trying to do everything right. I kept planning to talk to my Mentor and friend about the problem, but this constant struggle was keeping me busy—so very busy.

So, I made up my mind I was just going to have to try a little harder. I added some other things I thought would help: I started fasting twice a week; I started giving away all my money and my designer clothes and started wearing things I got from Goodwill. Still, there was so much stuff I couldn't seem to control, no matter how hard I worked at being a "good guy." And the people I was trying to be like... Well, I began to notice they weren't so hot either. In fact, I pretty much decided there was a lot of hypocrisy in the people I was working so hard to copy. What was the use?

I couldn't stand to be the way I was before but it certainly didn't help to pretend there were no struggles and that everything was OK. In desperation I flung myself across my bed—and cried.

You talk about a pity party? I had a major one.

"I can't do this anymore! I'm trying so hard to be good, to be godly, to do all the right things and it isn't working. I'm exhausted and angry that being a good person is so hard. What am I going to do?"

In the silence of my despair, I heard a quiet voice: "I thought you'd never ask."

I sat up and gathered my Goodwill rags around me, embarrassed that Someone was here with me in the deep recesses of my heart-house. Someone had already seen what a fraud I was. Someone knew how I was struggling to be what I would never be able to be by myself. I felt naked and exposed.

"Who are you?" I asked.

"I am your Comforter, your Teacher, the One Who pleads for you before the Father. I have lived here in your house for quite a while. Remember you did invite me in, and you gave me a key, but the place has been so crowded with your imitation 'good deeds' and, yes, your pride, that I've pretty much been relegated to that hall closet you never use.

"And the smell!" He said. "Really, the smell is awful. Let's open some windows and let in a little light and air. And the place is so crowded. Maybe we could take down some of these signs and get rid of these books of lists and schedules and meetings."

Gently the Comforter walked through my house and opened windows and cleared away my precious piles of activities and projects. He carried out all my fancy light fixtures (most of the bulbs were already burned out anyway) and suddenly I noticed that the rooms were filled with light and fragrance. At first I couldn't identify the source but then I realized it came from Him. And this is the really strange thing. Every time he touched me I had a little bit of that light and fragrance, as well.

Next he turned to me and said, "No wonder you are so exhausted. Somehow you have gotten yourself entangled in all these ropes and chains, and my goodness—what's this tape doing around your heart? It's a wonder you can even move. Don't you remember that Jesus died for you to release you from all this stuff?"

Why hadn't I even noticed? Fear was taped around my heart so that I could hardly breathe. Duty and pride and pretense were making sore places on my wrists and ankles.

"God hasn't given you the spirit of fear or these chains of bondage. When you became His He made you His own precious little child. All He requires of you is that you come to God and cry, 'Daddy, my Dear Father, help me!' You are trying to carry things that are His to carry."

Finally, He sat me down on the floor and gently rubbed sweet-smelling salve into the sore places my chains and tapes and ropes had made, and they were gone.

The next thing I knew He was washing my face and my hands and my feet so very, very gently. I can't tell you how clean and whole I felt. How very much at home and at rest!

I wanted to thank Him and apologize for the person I had been but I was speechless. Why had I carried this junk so long when it was so unnecessary? Why had I struggled so hard, when I had Someone to do what needed to be done and Who knew how to do it right?

I flung myself into His arms and rested my head on His shoulder. The thing is that I was so tired, so very tired and here was the rest I had been waiting for all my life!

"You know that I had prayed for you for a long time," the Comforter whispered in my ear. "Even when you were living your terrible life far away from the Father and the Rescue Center, I was the One Who was gently reminding you that there was hope and relief."

The tears began to roll down my cheeks. So many struggles to be happy! And so many struggles to be good!

"And," he continued, "I was praying for you even when you didn't know how to pray for yourself. I was so absorbed in your need that I carried my own groans and tears before the Father for you, because I knew how precious you were to Him."

All the time I was struggling, He had been gently pulling me toward Himself. It was His voice I had been hearing deep inside when I was in so much trouble, trying to make life turn out right my own way.

"So what do I do now?" I asked.

"Just listen to my voice. There will be changes in the way you live your life before others, but I will choose the changes. I will teach you what you need to know. I will speak to you and you will discover that the Word of God is coming alive to you in ways you've never seen before."

"But I tried to read the Bible—I even had a schedule—and it was so hard to keep up, so hard to understand."

He chuckled. "Of course you didn't understand. You got the Word of God all tangled up in your list of difficult duties and you squeezed all the sweetness out of it! You won't believe how much you are going to love it—how easy it will be to understand when you let Me be the Teacher!"

"This is almost too good to be true! Exciting but so restful too—to be able to just lean here on You and let You do the work. But what if other people don't understand? You know that some of the people at the Rescue Centers have pretty specific ideas about 'the rules.'"

"My dear child," the Teacher said. "The rules are there to remind you of how inadequate you are to be and to do what God requires of you. They aren't going to make you holy and happy and good. When you wake up every morning in my classroom, you will discover that my curriculum will work, my schedule will be orderly and doable and successful. You will have power and wisdom to do your work that you've never had before."

"But I tried so hard before…" I protested.

He put His finger on my mouth. "Shhhhh," he whispered. "Just listen to me…

"What you tried was 'behavior modification'; what I'm talking about is transformation.

If you'll let me work through your hands and feet and your mouth, you'll discover that you can have the power you need to be and to do what I have called you to be and to do. Just ask Me!"

"Wow! Power? You mean I can just say "Abracadabra! ...or something like that and have everything fall into place, everything turn out right?"

"Oh, my dear child! This Power is not to make your life easier and it certainly is not to make you look good. After all, this isn't about you; it's about doing the work of the Kingdom. It's all about the Father and the Son.

"When I gave my power at the Day of Pentecost, the effect was so profound that three thousand people turned their hearts to God!"

"I remember reading that. It must have been wonderful!" I said, "I wish I could have seen that you know, tongues of fire and different languages...and all those people saved..."

"It was wonderful, but you'll remember that those who had that power paid a price."

"Yea, I remember reading about that," I said. "Everybody thought they were drunk."

"Yes, and some of them were persecuted and some died. You remember Stephen, don't you? When he was martyred, his face glowed so that they could hardly look at him."

"That was you, wasn't it? That light in his face?"

"Yes, that was Me."

I got up and walked toward the window of my newly cleaned house. I could see the world out there and suddenly I was afraid. I wasn't sure what would happen when I stepped outside.

"Will you stay with me?" I asked anxiously.

"I will stay with you wherever you go. I will go with you through whatever you have to meet. I will help you with whatever you have to do. Don't be afraid."

Postscript:

These last weeks have been so wonderful; I wonder why I had known so little about my new friend. We talked about it together one evening over a cup of tea. (Well, I had tea, and He just sat by me and talked. I couldn't get enough of Him!)

"It's like everything is new," I said. "I wish I had gotten to know you a long time ago."

"I've been around a long time," He said. "Long before you knew me and long before those Christians at Pentecost saw my power."

"Actually, I took part in the creation of the world... I moved across the new universe, enjoying its beauty.

"I was the one Who gave gifts, and wisdom and power to the Old Testament saints—to priests, and prophets and kings. I even gave my gifts to the men who designed the tabernacle and the temple. (They were 'art teachers' you know; so many craftsmen they had to teach!) And don't forget that I'm involved anytime something beautiful is created. I make possible every scientific discovery, even great truth uncovered. Even when people do not know me or recognize where the gifts came from—I am the One who made it happen!

"I have spoken through a burning bush and even through the mouth of a donkey!

"I was in that great Cloud of Fire and Light when the Children of Israel traveled across the desert toward the Promised Land."

("Oh my," I thought. "That was some nightlight!")

"Yes," my Mentor said. "And I was the day-time Cloud that protected them from the desert sun and hid them from the enemies behind.

"Every miracle that has ever been performed, was done by my power; every illness cured, every victory won in a war, every mind restored, every wrong made right—I was there.

"Those who spoke or wrote down the Word of God did it through my power. Sometimes they didn't even know the meaning of what they wrote. They used their own words and they spoke in their own languages—but I was the One who told them what to say.

"I know all those whose hearts will turn to the Savior and I watch over them and lead them into truth; I give them the power to understand so they can receive the Gospel and I change their hearts from death to life.

"I am the One who gives conviction of sin—the One who gives assurance of salvation."

I interrupted here: "Are You the same as my conscience?"

"Heavens no!" He said. "I gave you a conscience but you can mess it up by ignoring sin. And unfortunately, you can also damage your conscience—like you did—by trying to earn your own way. When Christ died for you the point was to clean up your conscience from those old ideas. You know what I mean—thinking that you were smart enough or good enough to get to heaven your own way."

"Thank goodness," I sighed. "My conscience drove me crazy—no matter what I did!"

"Here's a little story that usually amazes people who first hear it. Can you imagine that I have inhabited even little babies who have not yet been born? Just check out the story of Samson's birth. And when Mary the mother of Jesus came to see her cousin Elizabeth who was pregnant with John the Baptist, both of us jumped for joy in Elizabeth's womb!

"Now you have a 'real' job to do," my friend said. "You know this grace I've given you? Now you go show it to those other people down at the rescue center. And that dark world out there needs to see my grace in you. I love them too, you know!

"And here's another thing," he said. "This is a mystery you probably won't understand, but when Jesus Christ died, I hovered over His precious body and I was involved in His Resurrection. The Father's will is My will and Christ's work was My work as well."

(One side note by the human writer of this dialogue: Some of you have lost people you love recently. Let me give you a word of comfort. If the Holy Spirit is involved in the Resurrection process, is it possible that when our loved ones in Christ die and are buried, their precious remains are watched over by the Holy Spirit waiting for the day of Resurrection?)

So, that's my story—how the Holy Spirit came to live at my house and finally took control.

He would like to come and live with you too—maybe He already does but it's possible you've put Him in some spare corner of the house.

Where can you find Him? The Bible is His address book. Just read it with your eyes and heart open and you'll find Him everywhere! (© 2012 by Jessie Rice Sandberg)

But this precious treasure—this light and power that now shine within us—is held in a perishable container, that is, in our weak bodies. Everyone can see that the glorious power within must be from God and is not our own. (2 Cor. 4:7, TLB)

[Jesus speaking to His disciples before His death:] If you love me, you will keep my commandments. And I will ask the Father, and he will give you another Helper, to be with you forever, even the Spirit of truth, whom the world cannot receive, because it neither sees him nor knows him. You know him, for he dwells with you and will be in you. (John 14:15–17)

There is therefore now no condemnation for those who are in Christ Jesus. For the law of the Spirit of life has set you free in Christ Jesus from the law of sin and death. For God has done what the law, weakened by the flesh, could not do. By sending his own Son in the likeness of sinful flesh and for sin, he condemned sin in the flesh, in order that the righteous requirement of the law might be fulfilled in us, who walk not according to the flesh but according to the Spirit. (Rom. 8:1–4)

For all who are led by the Spirit of God are children of God. So you should not be like cowering, fearful slaves. You should behave instead like God's very own children, adopted into his family—calling him "Father, dear Father"; For his Holy Spirit speaks to us deep in our hearts and tells us that we are God's children. And since we are his children, we will share his treasures— for everything God gives to his Son Christ, is ours too. But if we are to share his glory, we must also share his suffering. (Rom. 8:14–18)

And the Holy Spirit helps us in our distress. For we don't even know what we should pray for, nor how we should pray. But the Holy Spirit prays for us with groanings that cannot be expressed in words. And the Father who knows all hearts knows what the Spirit is saying for the Spirit pleads for us believers in harmony with God's own will. (Rom. 8:26–27)

But then God our Savior shows us his kindness and love. He saved us, not because of the good things we did, but because of his mercy. He washed away our sins and gave us new life through the Holy Spirit. He generously poured out the Spirit upon us because of what Jesus Christ our Savior did. He declared us not guilty because of his great kindness. And now we know that we will inherit eternal life. (Titus 3:4–7)

I appeal to you therefore, brothers, by the mercies of God, to present your bodies as a living sacrifice, holy and acceptable to God, which is your spiritual worship. Do not be conformed to this world, but be transformed by the renewal of your mind, that by testing you may discern what is the will of God, what is good and acceptable and perfect. (Rom. 12:1–2)

The people in the church had welcomed me and loved me, but Satan was attacking my mind and my heart. Would they still feel the same if they knew my past? I was content with not knowing for sure rather than risking the possible outcome, but God had a different plan for my life.

The ladies from the church were attending a ladies' retreat at Camp Barakel, a church camp in Fairview, Michigan. I was asked to attend and thrilled to be included. We had a lot of fun—canoed down the Au Sable River, walked in the woods, popcorn in the evenings, and fireplaces in the chapel with the fire burning 24/7. It was definitely a warm, inviting, comfortable, and safe place to be. I felt very at home there and close to the Lord.

The guest speaker that weekend was Jessie Rice Sandberg. I knew she was from the South because of her accent. She appeared to be kind, gentle, trusting, and tenderhearted. She sure knew the Word of God. I enjoyed listening to her and how she talked about the God of the Bible. After one of the sessions, I found myself sitting by the fireplace, not wanting to leave. Everyone else had left for the dining hall for dinner. Usually, I never skipped a meal and was always in line when it was time to eat, but at this moment, eating was the furthest thing from my mind.

I was sitting by the fireplace when Jessie came in and sat beside me. We talked for several minutes, mostly about small stuff. She seemed, in person, the same as I envisioned her while she was speaking from the pulpit, yet as we talked, I learned several other qualities about her. She was loving, trusting, safe, and deeply cared about people. Anyone who knows anything about Jessie Rice Sandberg knows she is going to get around to asking about your relationship with the Lord, and she asked me. By then, I knew Jessie was from Augusta, Georgia, and I would probably never see her again. I could have easily said I was a Christian, enjoyed serving in the church, and been done. Looking back, I know it was the Lord who drew me to her. Before I knew it, I had shared all the Lord had done in my heart for me and the lifestyle from which He had delivered me. With tear-filled eyes and a gentle spirit, sharing my joy, she hugged me and said, "I love you."

"By this all people will know that you are my disciples, if you have love for one another" (John 13:35). Jessie certainly demonstrated being a true disciple of God's grace. God gave me a genuine true friend that day. As far as me never seeing her again, it's been thirty years since that day, and I still see her and talk with her often. Jessie has been a sincere friend, mentor, and great encouragement to me in my Christian walk. I might also add she has been very instrumental in me taking on the task of writing this book.

One thing I have learned is it is much easier to submit to God's will sooner than later. If you are a true believer, He will ultimately have His way with you.

The Sunday school class I was attending was taught by Earlene Lindsay, the pastor's wife. I learned so much in that class as we studied God's Word together. I grew to love Earlene and all the ladies, and they returned that love to me. Our Sunday school class was doing seven-minute testimonies. Each Sunday, a lady would voluntarily share what God had done in her life. Key word here is *voluntarily*. I loved hearing from the ladies and the amazing things God had done.

On the way home from church one Sunday, Lois and I were talking about the class and the testimonies from each individual person and their life. Lois then said to me, "You should consider sharing what God has done for you."

Before she even finished talking, I immediately brought my car to a stop in the middle of Opdyke Road. "I will *never* do that!" I said firmly and determined. Up until that point, I had kept that a secret. I was not willing to open old wounds of rejection and shame by sharing my sin. I had wrestled with that statement for several days and nights, asking myself why I would even think about jeopardizing the friendships I have made within the church. In my heart, I had believed my sin was far worse than anything I had ever heard.

Being convicted, and submissive, I agreed to share my testimony with Earlene first (before sharing with the class). In the back of my mind, I was 99 percent sure Earlene Lindsay was not going to consider my testimony before the women since my sin was "worse" than any other that had been shared. Earlene and I agreed to meet between Sunday school and church, and ten minutes turned into an hour and a half! After eagerly listening to my story, Earlene responded by saying, "I can't wait for you to share this with the ladies."

Earlene had taught a class outside our church at Waterford Community Church. I'm sure by her asking me to share at another location prior to my home church, Earlene was guarding me and giving me opportunity. Upon completion of my sharing at Waterford Community Church, I remember we sang "Victory in Jesus," and what a victory it was. Several of the ladies approached me, handing me notes requesting prayer for their sons, daughters, or loved ones. One lady came up and hugged me, saying, "You don't know who I am." I responded no, and she then revealed she was the mother of a young man I had dated in high school. She had known me since I was a teenager and shared in my joy of what God had done.

I left encouraged because now the ladies knew and still accepted me. I took a blind step in obedience, and God led me to a giant step in His grace and mercy. He was faithful and showed me the way to even greater obedience and opportunities to share His love, grace, mercy, and forgiveness (even for the worse sin). "I can do all things through him who strengthens me" (Phil. 4:13).

Is God enough for such a time as this?

Chapter 8
Unchartered Waters

> But he said to me, "My grace is sufficient for you, for my power is made perfect in weakness." Therefore I will boast all the more gladly of my weaknesses, so that the power of Christ may rest upon me.
>
> —2 Corinthians 12:9

I love being around the water. The peaceful sound of a flowing river, the lake in the early morning as it appears to be a sheet of glass with fog settling just above it, and the oceans with the waves crashing into the piers as the sun sets magnificently all along the horizon are all just glimpses of heaven, and it is soothing to my soul.

I have a list of fifty things I want to do before I die. The problem is I keep adding new things to them, and I'll probably need to live to be 110 to accomplish them all. No, jumping out an airplane with a parachute is not one of them.

My grandparents lived on Black Lake in Michigan. Ever since I can remember, my sister and I have spent our summers always in our bathing suits and mostly in the water. I loved everything about the lake. Fishing, swimming, canoeing, and skiing—we did it all. Even as a child, I wanted to race hydroplanes that skimmed across the top of the water. That all ended after watching a hydroplane roll several times during a race.

One of the latest things added to my list was tubing. They didn't have such a thing when I was growing up, so at the age of sixty-six, I finally got to do that and cross it off my list. Yes, it was fun! While on the tube, it didn't take me long to realize the person driving the boat had much more control over me and my tube than I did. Fortunately, I knew the person behind the wheel. Not only was Scott a pastor; his mother, my friend Barb, was also on a tube next to me being pulled at the same time. I was sure he wasn't going to do anything crazy. I also learned if I tried to go against the boat and direction of the driver, it would end up a disaster. Much like when we go against God's will in our lives.

When we as believers surrender our all to Christ, that means dying to self daily. "And whoever does not take his cross and follow me is not worthy of me. Whoever finds his life will lose it, and whoever loses his life for my sake will find it" (Matt. 10:38–39). The desire of my heart was to be obedient and serve Him the best I could, with much help from the Holy Spirit, of course. Without that, it would be an impossible task—one I was about to discover. Sharing my past was not something I was comfortable with. Believe me, I didn't go knocking on any doors. Even now, as I write this, there are only four people I have told voluntarily without being asked. I can honestly say it was only done by the prompting of the Holy Spirit. I continue to keep that part of my past guarded and very much a secret. Enter God and His will…

I soon received a letter from my friend, Jessie—the friend I met at Camp Barakel. This was before computers and e-mail. In the letter, she asked if I could write my testimony so it could be published in *The Joyful Woman*, a magazine for and about Bible-believing women who want God's best in their lives. I prayed about sharing and wanted to be obedient to the Lord's leading. I agreed, knowing deep inside nobody will want to read or even talk about it. So that would be that—over and done in my mind! After the article was published, Jessie contacted me, asking if I would be willing to come and share my testimony at the Joyful Woman Jubilee, a Christian women's conference they sponsored once a year in Chattanooga, Tennessee. *"Are you kidding me?"* was my first reaction. I could come up with many good excuses why I should say no, but there was one very good reason I should agree: God. Since it had been several years since I invited Christ into my life as Lord of my life, I wanted to obey. "The heart of a man plans his way, but the Lord establishes his steps" (Prov. 16:9).

What I have found is whenever God asks me to do something, He is always faithful to work in and through me to help me obey and serve Him. It was a step of obedience tied to a whole lot of faith that I wrote back to Jessie and agreed to share my testimony. When I received the program, I noticed a lady named Kay Arthur was to be the keynote speaker. I read she and her husband were founders of Precept Ministries. I also read she authored many books and Bible studies. That was all I knew of her, and I was looking forward to meeting her and hearing her speak.

Lois and several ladies from my church made the trip with me. They were a great encouragement, for sure. The jubilee started Thursday evening and continued through Saturday afternoon. I wasn't scheduled to speak until Saturday morning, which was very difficult. I would have preferred to do it and get it over with. I have never been good at waiting, but I rested in the fact that God's timing was always perfect. Thursday evening was the opening and introduction of speakers. By that time, everyone was able to identify me as the one whom God delivered from the homosexual lifestyle. It was not only in the program but also printed right next to my picture. Kay Arthur was not there that evening but was scheduled to speak the next morning.

Arriving at the auditorium Friday morning, Bev, one of my friends who came to support me, grabbed my arm in a concerned voice and said, "Margaret, look at all these people."

Up until then, I hadn't noticed the number of people attending. At that moment, I began to question God. "Are you sure about this?" I was the kid who found a reason to stay home from school when oral book reports were due. "Lord," I prayed. "You are going to have to show up—big time!"

Was I scared? Absolutely! I did know in my heart it was God who orchestrated this, and I held on tightly to the promise: "I can do all things through him who strengthens me" (Phil. 4:13). Did He show up? Absolutely! I remember being calm and sure. My friend, that could only come from God. What I recall most were the women who approached me, clinging to me, saying, "Thank you for telling the truth and giving me hope." Everyone who approached me was concerned for their son, daughter, or other acquaintances. Yes, there is hope. No one is so deep in sin that the blood of Christ did not cover and the love of that same Savior cannot reach. What a blessing to know God would use the road of my past to comfort and show others the way to Christ and, therefore, to glorify Him.

> Blessed be God, even the Father of our Lord Jesus Christ, the Father of mercies, and the God of all comfort; Who comforteth us in all our tribulation, that we may be able to comfort them which are in any trouble, by the comfort wherewith we ourselves are comforted of God. For as the sufferings of Christ abound in us, so our consolation also aboundeth by Christ. And whether we be afflicted, it is for your consolation and salvation, which is effectual in the enduring of the same sufferings which we also suffer: or whether we be comforted, it is for your consolation and salvation. And our hope of you is steadfast, knowing, that as ye are partakers of the sufferings, so shall ye be also of the consolation." (2 Cor. 1:3–7, KJV)

This was the call to travel in "uncharted waters," although I didn't know it at the time. I was encouraged, and my heart was glad to offer hope and be a blessing to others. Little did I know the power of Satan and his planned attack would come against me from those I had trusted.

Is God enough for such a time as this?

Chapter 9
Identifying with Christians

> For I am not ashamed of the gospel, for it is the power of God for salvation to everyone who believes, to the Jew first and also to the Greek. For in it the righteousness of God is revealed from faith for faith, as it is written, "The righteous shall live by faith."
>
> —Romans 1:16–17

Many of us—whether in work, school, sports, or charities—wear a uniform. This identifies us with a particular group of people. The most recognized uniforms are probably tied to sports. Each team has their own specific colors and logos. Fans proudly wear a jersey in support of their favorite team. All one needs to do is observe apparel on any given day, and they would know what team a person is rooting for and, most likely, who their favorite player happens to be. Have you ever noticed how many people wear a cross? I recently read from *Sparkling Gems from the Greek*, written by Rick Renner.

> When I read about the crucifixion of Jesus, it makes me want to repent from the callousness with which the world looks upon the cross today. In our society, the cross has become a fashion item, decorated with gems, rhinestones, gold, and silver. Beautiful crosses of jewelry adorn women's ears and dangle at the bottom of gold

chains and necklaces. The symbol of the cross is even tattooed on people's flesh!

The reason this is so disturbing to me is that in beautifying the cross to make it pleasing to look upon, people have forgotten that it wasn't beautiful or lavishly decorated at all. In fact, the cross of Jesus was shocking and appalling.

I do wear a cross around my neck. I never hide it or cover it up. Not that I need to be reminded of the work Jesus did on the cross, but more so, it is to identify to anyone who recognizes it that I am a Christian. My sins are forgiven because of that cross, and I'm a child of the King. "The Spirit himself bears witness with our spirit that we are children of God" (Rom. 8:16).

Christ endured the cross out of obedience to His father and His love for me. Yes, the cross may be a piece of jewelry, a picture, or even a piece of wood sitting on top of a steeple, but that symbol is where I met my Lord. It is quite obvious the meaning isn't the same to everyone. Often, when I see someone wearing a cross, I'll ask, "Oh, are you a Christian? I see you are wearing a cross."

You'd be surprised how many times the response was "No, I just thought it was cool" or "It was a gift." Mine was also a gift, but I know it wasn't given because it was in style. It was given because of the change in my life and the new example of my lifestyle. The best way I can describe it is through the words of the old hymn: "So, I'll cherish the Old Rugged Cross 'til my trophies at last I lay down. I will cling to the Old Rugged Cross and exchange it someday for a crown."

I am single and identify and bond mostly with single women, although I have many friends who are married. Soon God led me to another group of people with whom I connected and identified. They are called SOLOS (Serving Others Loving Our Savior).

In the late summer of 1989, Jessie invited twenty-five single women to a weekend meeting at her home in Augusta, Georgia. Eighteen women from all over the country accepted the invitation to a retreat for "single Christian professional women." Reservations were made for them at a local historic inn, but the meetings and meals were in Jessie's home. She and her husband, Don, prepared and served the meals, and Jessie led the sessions. Most of the women didn't know anyone else in the room before that meeting. Eighteen women looked each other over and wondered if they had anything in common or if they had an interest in knowing one another better. Some were widowed; some divorced. Others had never been married. There was a missionary, several nurses, a few teachers, a chemist, a postal worker, and a smattering of various other job titles.

Jessie and Don tried to make everyone welcomed and loved, but it wasn't until the last session of the weekend that the Holy Spirit started to break down walls and began to knit hearts together. When asked if the group wanted to meet again next year, they decided they did. Jessie again made all the preparations for the retreat in 1990 at Watts Bar Dam State Park in Tennessee, but she let us know then if this was something we wanted to continue, we would have to do the work ourselves in the future and recommended we elect officers.

One special memory from Watts Bar Dam was the woman who came into the park restaurant while we were having lunch. She asked about our group, so we invited her to our next session. She accepted, and before the day was over, Libby Hanford, Jessie's sister, had led her to the Lord. We never saw her again, but she later wrote she had been hurting so much that day that she had decided to commit suicide. Now that she had the Lord in her life, that plan had been scrapped.

Several changes were made before the next meeting. We decided "Single Christian Professional Women" was a little wordy, so we adopted SOLOS: Serving Others, Loving Our Savior.

These ladies are incredible and unique, much like our founders, Jessie and Don Sandberg. The Lord has used SOLOS to change lives, encourage others, and bring honor and glory to Himself. We do crazy things sometimes. When several of us get together, we often stay up until two in the morning just talking or playing games. That's a tough one for me since I'm not a night person. We have parties for no reason, talent shows, and have even been known to make snow angels and snowmen for shut-ins. That occurs mostly in the north. Neither would survive in Chattanooga or South Carolina. We drop off a poinsettia to a shut-in and make chicken noodle soup for a neighbor who is sick or just sit with them.

Recently, Julia, one of the SOLOS and a dear friend, was flying home to Chattanooga and had a three-hour layover in Detroit, arriving at five in the afternoon. I decided to meet her at the airport and have a cup of coffee and an egg and sausage biscuit. We had a chance to catch up on each other's lives and share our hearts. That's what SOLOS do—they love, listen, assist, and care about people. It is a great group of women I am thankful to be a part of. They truly express and display the love of Christ. Yes, SOLOS did know of my past and the sin from which God had delivered me. I was a sinner saved by grace just like all people who come to believe in Jesus Christ. The SOLOS verse is: "For I know the plans I have for you, declares the LORD, plans for welfare and not for evil, to give you a future and a hope" (Jer. 29:11).

It was important for me to belong to a church. Remember, the church is not a building but a body of believers—God's people. It is a part of the Christian walk.

> And let us consider how to stir up one another
> to love and good works, not neglecting to meet
> together, as is the habit of some, but encouraging
> one another, and all the more as you see the Day
> drawing near. (Heb. 10:24–25)

It brought me great joy attending and serving at church. Most of the congregation didn't know of my past; still it isn't something I share easily. Even when prompted by the Holy Spirit, I'm often reluctant. Satan did have a field day in this area of my life. If they knew of the horrible sin of my past, I was sure they would withdraw their love and support. God has forgiven my sins "as far as the east is from the west, so far does he remove our transgressions from us" (Ps. 103:12). Surely, God's people who have His grace, love, and mercy freely given in their lives are capable and called to express the same to fellow believers. I wanted desperately to seek God's will for my life. The verse I memorized and clung to was:

> I appeal to you therefore, brothers, by the mercies of God, to present your bodies as a living sacrifice, holy and acceptable to God, which is your spiritual worship. Do not be conformed to this world, but be transformed by the renewal of your mind, that by testing you may discern what is the will of God, what is good and acceptable and perfect. (Rom. 12:1–2)

It didn't take long before God revealed His will and direction. Precept Ministries had contacted me to be a guest on Kay Arthur's radio program. Out of obedience, Lois and I traveled to Chattanooga to meet with Kay and tape my testimony. I remember it as if it were yesterday. I was totally nervous. I knew it was God who brought me there, and I knew He would be faithful.

Kay and her husband had just returned from vacation. Kay walked in to greet us still wearing her vacation clothes—a sweatshirt and blue jeans. She was also sipping on tomato soup from a Tupperware bowl. A sense of calmness came about me as I realized she was a human being saved by grace just like me. The program was aired, and many responded with questions as the topic of homosexuality is seldom discussed. After that, I had several opportunities to work with Kay. She is truly a godly lady and wonderful teacher who knows and loves God's Word. I have learned so much from her. The Inductive Bible Studies from Precepts are great tools and resources for Christians. I was encouraged and blessed to help others who had friends or loved ones trapped in this lifestyle.

Everything was going smoothly until my next trip to Chattanooga. The Joyful Woman had asked me to return and share what God had been doing in my life during a workshop at the jubilee. While in the hospitality room, I overhead the women in charge of the jubilee asking why certain churches didn't attend. It sounded as though they were faithful and attended every year. "It's because Margaret is here and sharing her testimony. They chose not to come."

Seriously? I expected opposition but not from within the church, especially God's people. I hadn't even spoken yet, but what I really wanted to do was pack my bags and go home. I guess you could say I was blindsided. I surely didn't see that coming. As I walked out the room into the sanctuary, a lady met me at the door, shaking and in tears. She spoke the words: "I'm here because you are here." The fear and resentment I felt seconds before seemed to fade quickly. My heart and mind was now focused on the lady gripping my hands in desperation. She had just found out her daughter was convinced God had made her gay, and she was going to pursue that lifestyle. The mother's heart was broken, which in turn broke my heart. We sat, talked, and prayed together. As she left, she spoke these words that are embedded on the walls of my heart: "Thank you for speaking the truth and giving me hope that God can forgive and transform the life of anyone, even the homosexual."

I soon began to meet opposition at home. Our pastor was preaching on Romans chapter 1, addressing the sin of homosexuality. He asked me if I would share my testimony with the church, and I agreed, only to find out the deacon board would not approve. Excuse me? Is there something I'm not doing right? I began to search the scriptures to determine where I had failed.

As First John 1:9 says, I had confessed my sins. God had cleansed me from all unrighteousness. My desire and daily prayer was:

> You shall love the Lord your God with all your heart and with all your soul and with all your mind. This is the great and first commandment. And a second is like it: You shall love your neighbor as yourself. (Matt. 22:37–39)

Our ultimate goal as Christians is to bring honor and glory to Him. With the help of the Holy Spirit, I was trying to live that out in my life. The standards seemed to be different for me. Had I committed a sin greater than any other? Ready to leave the church, I talked with my friend, Jessie, as I often do when I need to sort through things. After listening to me kick and scream for several minutes, she calmly asked, "Where are you going to go?" Then she stated, "I have news for you. There is no perfect church."

Opposition and disappointment would continue to pop their heads. Maybe it's not proper, but I call them the Pharisees in my life. I pray for them and also that God would work in my heart. I am responsible for myself, my words, and my actions. So often I recite the Serenity Prayer by Reinhold Niebuhr: "God grant me the serenity to accept the things I cannot change, courage to change things I can, and wisdom to know the difference."

God often brings to mind the lady I met in Chattanooga, her life turned upside down by the devastating news from her daughter who wanted to pursue the homosexual lifestyle. All of us have been in that place when everything in life seems to unravel, and we are overtaken by uncertainty and fear. In the midst of that storm, we need to remember we are not alone. Our faithful Shepherd is there. He is the same yesterday, today, and forever.

> The LORD is my shepherd; I shall not want. He makes me lie down in green pastures. He leads me beside still waters. He restores my soul. He leads me in paths of righteousness for his name's sake. Even though I walk through the valley of the shadow of death, I will fear no evil, for you are with me; your rod and your staff, they comfort me. You prepare a table before me in the presence of my enemies; you anoint my head with oil; my cup overflows. Surely goodness and mercy shall follow me all the days of my life, and I shall dwell in the house of the LORD forever. (Ps. 23)

Is God enough for such a time as this?

Chapter 10
Silence

And Jesus came and said to them, "All authority
in heaven and on earth has been given to me.
Go therefore and make disciples of all nations,
baptizing them in the name of the Father and
of the Son and of the Holy Spirit, teaching
them to observe all that I have commanded
you. And behold, I am with you always, to the
end of the age."

—Matthew 28:18–20

Remember the old saying "If you can't say something nice about someone, it's better not to say anything at all"? Many of us have that mastered. We don't want to be unkind or critical. We think it's none of our business, and we certainly don't want to offend someone.

There are many times we do need to keep our mouth shut. I try very hard to think before I speak in certain situations or else I might eat my words later. Sometimes I just need to listen. I find it hard to talk and listen at the same time.

Some of you may remember a song back in the sixties cowritten by Bob Gaudio of the American band the Four Seasons with their producer, Bob Crow. The title was "Silence is Golden, but My Eyes Still See." Yes, silence is golden sometimes, but now is not the time to be silent. We, as Christians, are called to stand up for what is truth and proclaim the Gospel of Jesus Christ. We are not able to proclaim anything while we are silent. The church has been silent for a long time now. It's legal to murder an unborn child while in the mother's womb, which is okay in the eyes of society but not in God's eyes. For years, the word *homosexual* was never spoken in society, not to mention from behind a pulpit. Now same-sex marriage is the law of the land. This is legal, but it is not acceptable in God's eyes.

Since the lesbian, gay, bisexual, transgender, and queer (LGBTQ) movement was founded in 1989, one of their main goals was to change marriage as we know it today. They have succeeded, and they are not finished. Why have they succeeded? Because they gathered together, spoke loudly, and never gave up.

A wise writer once said, "Tolerance is the virtue of people who do not believe in anything." Dr. James Dobson said in his family newsletter dated July 1998, "When we become so accommodating of evil that we neither recognize it nor oppose it, our moral collapse is imminent." It's been twenty years since Dr. Dobson wrote that in his newsletter. I think most Christians, myself included, would agree as a nation, our moral collapse is no longer imminent—it has already happened. We have arrived! We are right where Scripture states:

> But understand this, that in the last days there will come times of difficulty. For people will be lovers of self, lovers of money, proud, arrogant, abusive, disobedient to their parents, ungrateful, unholy, heartless, unappeasable, slanderous, without self-control, brutal, not loving good, treacherous, reckless, swollen with conceit, lovers of pleasure rather than lovers of God, having the appearance of godliness, but denying its power. Avoid such people. For among them are those who creep into households and capture weak women, burdened with sins and led astray by various passions, always learning and never able to arrive at a knowledge of the truth. (2 Tim. 3:1–7)

Dr. Dobson and Focus on the Family took much criticism in taking a stand for family and speaking the truth in love and always with compassion. They were referred to as "religious nuts, far-right extremists, and fundamentalists." They were being attacked for defending what they believed: God's Word.

Someone has said, "The only thing necessary for the triumph of evil is that good men do nothing." People in church have accepted tolerance, political correctness, and "I'm okay, you're okay." I saw a bumper sticker recently that read "Pray that God would be more tolerant." Wow! We have become so wise in our own minds that some think they can change the heart, soul, and mind of the almighty God. "I am the Alpha and the Omega, the first and the last, the beginning and the end" (Rev. 22:13).

I probably sound like I'm ranting and raving right now. That's because I am. I promised my brother Rick I would try very hard not to do that. It is in these times I find it very difficult, if not impossible. Just when you think you've heard it all, something more ridiculous happens. Like when the Supreme Court legalized same-sex marriage—in other words, legalizing sin again. Abortion is now legal, same-sex marriage is now legal, sin is now legal. What's sad is people are not only being silent but also agreeing with much of what is taking place. It seems we tend to know God's Word and believe it to be true until darkness and sin creep into our families, group of friends, and even the church itself.

Several years ago, a book was written, *Prayers for Bobby*, and later became a movie. It was the story of a mother coming to terms with the suicide of her gay son. Mary Griffith's son, Bobby, jumped from a bridge into the path of a tractor trailer, taking his life at the age of twenty. It was said he had everything to live for yet took his life in reaction to the rejection of his lifestyle from his family and society. When Mary, Bobby's mother, learned of her son's lifestyle, she was devastated, as most parents would be. She believed in God and often took her kids to church. Desperately, she tried to fix Bobby. She would leave written scripture around the house and over the bathroom mirrors—verses that pertained to her son's choice of lifestyle, like either of the following:

> Cease to hear instruction, my son, and you will
> stray from the words of knowledge. (Prov. 19:27)

> Little children, let no one deceive you. Whoever practices righteousness is righteous, as he is righteous. Whoever makes a practice of sinning is of the devil, for the devil has been sinning from the beginning. The reason the Son of God appeared was to destroy the works of the devil. (1 John 3:7–8)

It stated in the book she searched the Bible for appropriate verses. She sought out Christian counselors and found books to push on Bobby to read. Mary would say to her son, "Bobby, we can beat this if we just trust in God." Or she would say, "Homosexuality is curable with God's help. We've seen it on television, remember? It's not a natural thing. God will help you weed it out, healing through prayers. That's the good news, Bobby!"

Mary believed with total faith God was adamant about the abomination of homosexuality and would not be so diabolical as to fail to cure her son. However, Jesus Himself warns of false prophets and those who have been deceived.

> Not everyone who says to me, "Lord, Lord," will enter the kingdom of heaven, but the one who does the will of my Father who is in heaven. On that day many will say to me, "Lord, Lord, did we not prophesy in your name, and cast out demons in your name, and do many mighty works in your name?" And then will I declare to them, "I never knew you; depart from me, you workers of lawlessness." (Matt. 7:21–23)
>
> So God created mankind in his own image, in the image of God he created them; male and female he created them. God blessed them and said to them, "Be fruitful and increase in number; fill the earth and subdue it. Rule over the fish in the sea and the birds in the sky and over

every living creature that moves on the ground."
(Gen. 1:27–28, NIV)

The LORD God said, "It is not good for the
man to be alone. I will make a helper suitable
for him." So the LORD God caused the man to
fall into a deep sleep; and while he was sleeping,
he took one of the man's ribs and then closed up
the place with flesh. Then the LORD God made
a woman from the rib he had taken out of the
man, and he brought her to the man. The man
said, "This is now bone of my bones and flesh
of my flesh; she shall be called 'woman,' for she
was taken out of man." That is why a man leaves
his father and mother and is united to his wife,
and they become one flesh. Adam and his wife
were both naked, and they felt no shame. (Gen.
2:18, 21–25, NIV)

All of Mary's efforts failed, and shortly, Bobby took his own
life. Just as sad as losing a son was the fact that she turned from the
one true God of the Bible to the gay church that teaches false doctrine. Mary became a spokesperson for PFLAG (Parents, Families,
and Friends of Lesbians and Gays).

I myself have attended the gay church searching for God and
His truth and guidance. I found the teaching of the gay church does
not line up with God's Word. "And this is the testimony, that God
gave us eternal life, and this life is in his Son. Whoever has the Son
has life; whoever does not have the Son of God does not have life" (1
John 5:11–12).

One doesn't have to look far to find a church that is accommodating. They tickle your ears and tell you God loves you and wants
you to be happy. All is well. Be cautious, God warns us in His Word.

For the time is coming when people will not
endure sound teaching, but having itching ears
they will accumulate for themselves teachers to

suit their own passions, and will turn away from listening to the truth and wander off into myths. (2 Tim. 4:3–4)

Many choose to reject God completely. Then there are those who try their hardest to mold God to fit the lifestyle they have chosen—like an add-on.

God demands all our heart. Jesus said, "No one can serve two masters; for either he will hate the one and love the other, or he will be devoted to one and despise the other. You cannot serve God and wealth" (Matt. 6:24, NASB).

The first of the Ten Commandments is "You shall have no other gods before me" (Exod. 20:3).

Is God enough for such a time as this?

Chapter 11
Standing Firm for the Gospel of Christ

A man of many companions may come to ruin, but there is a friend who sticks closer than a brother.

—Proverbs 18:24

Not long ago, things were more black and white than they are today. Murder, adultery, stealing, lying, homosexuality, and taking the Lord's name in vain were all considered sin and just plain wrong. Now the black and white is a gray area, and the definite line we dare not cross has become—to say the least—blurred.

According to the World Health Organization, there are over three thousand abortions per day in the United States. When I went to school decades ago, girls who became pregnant while in school could not participate in graduation ceremonies. Adultery now is not even spoken of as adultery; it's simply just an affair. I guess that makes it less evil in the eyes of the one committing the sin. Stealing is not stealing but merely fraud. Even lying on our tax form is done by the majority, and that makes it all right. In college today, we have Homosexuality 101 offered as a class. Using the Lord's name in vain has become common as an everyday language, without any consideration of the true meaning of who God is.

There are no distinct lines in right or wrong—everything goes and everybody's doing it. The word *sin* has seemingly disappeared not only in society but also even in our churches. "I'm okay, you're okay." Remember that phrase? We are being deceived, and Satan is doing a great job.

> Now therefore fear the LORD and serve him in sincerity and in faithfulness. Put away the gods that your fathers served beyond the River and in Egypt, and serve the LORD. And if it is evil in your eyes to serve the LORD, choose this day whom you will serve, whether the gods your fathers served in the region beyond the River, or the gods of the Amorites in whose land you dwell. But as for me and my house, we will serve the LORD. (Josh. 24:14–15)

There is no riding the fence. If we choose to love, honor, obey, and serve the Lord, there will be a price to pay. It isn't an easy thing taking a stand for truth—God's truth! I believe the Bible to be the inerrant Word of God.

> All Scripture is breathed out by God and profitable for teaching, for reproof, for correction, and for training in righteousness, that the man of God may be complete, equipped for every good work. (2 Tim. 3:16–17)

For me, it was one thing to know the Word of God yet altogether different when living it out. Jesus Himself said, "If you love me, you will keep my commandments" (John 14:15). Some commandments are easier and more natural for me than others. For instance, love, mercy, grace, giving, and forgiveness are all definite marks of a true Christian (just to name a few). I love people, and expressing that love by giving, caring, and showing mercy and forgiveness is a part of who I am. This is part of who I was even before I came to know Jesus Christ as my savior. Because of the love Jesus showed me and all sinners, this became more an act of love rather than a tool to be accepted by others.

74

One of the more difficult commandments for me is confrontation. That is not an easy thing to do, yet Scripture is clear of our obligation to our brothers and sisters in Christ in order to restore them to the faith: "Brothers, if anyone is caught in any transgression, you who are spiritual should restore him in a spirit of gentleness. Keep watch on yourself, lest you too be tempted" (Gal. 6:1). When we see a brother or sister in Christ committing or living in sin, we are to confront them in love.

The church I had been attending had issues in their leadership by allowing a practicing homosexual to participate in ministry within the church. I struggled with this for a long time as it broke my heart, and I became very disturbed. I wanted to just leave and find another church. There were several local churches I would have been very happy in attending, but God convicted me to confront the situation with the leadership instead of running away from it. After much prayer and godly counsel, I confronted the person who was being permitted to lead in ministry within the church. The pastor and his wife, who were also this person's parents, were present, making the situation much more difficult. Even more heartbreaking is the fact that all these people are long-time friends. I had my Bible with me and asked the young man if he believed the Bible to be the authoritative word of God. "Yes," he responded. More surprising than his answer was the fact that he did not try to discredit the Scripture or even justify his lifestyle. He knew it was sin, simply stating, "This is the way I want to live." Several Scripture verses ran through my mind. One of them was:

> No one born of God makes a practice of sinning, for God's seed abides in him; and he cannot keep on sinning, because he has been born of God. By this it is evident who are the children of God, and who are the children of the devil: whoever does not practice righteousness is not of God, nor is the one who does not love his brother. (1 John 3:9–10)

My heart was sad that day as he got up from the table and walked away satisfied in his choice of lifestyle. I did what was asked of me—I confronted and warned the young man of the sinful path he had chosen.

That was not the end; only the beginning. Sin had been disregarded in this church for some time and never confronted. All was well, or so it seemed. We were doing all the right things: helping the needy, distributing food and clothing to anyone in need, reaching out to the community, and offering Bible study classes, weekend retreats, and family camp. But we were simply playing church. Sin was evident in the body.

The situation with Ryan, the pastor's son, caused much dissention and uneasiness within the church. People were talking amongst themselves about what was happening. Many times, we as Christians know what the Word of God says about the way we live, what's acceptable, and what's not, until sin hits home. It creeps in, and all of a sudden, what we once believed as absolute truth is now shaken. The Word is not clear any longer, and we find ways to justify our loved ones' choices. I can understand the world through its darkened eyes going down that path. However, it is more difficult for me to understand a fellow believer who is either caught in an unacceptable, sinful lifestyle or supporting a person in the choice they have made because of the family, friend, or parent-child relationship. It's in this situation we find ourselves in a most uncomfortable place.

Remember this statement, fellow believer. This is important because if you claim to be a follower of Christ and He lives in your heart, you cannot walk in darkness.

> This is the message we have heard from him and proclaim to you, that God is light, and in him is no darkness at all. If we say we have fellowship with him while we walk in darkness, we lie and do not practice the truth. But if we walk in the light, as he is in the light, we have fellowship with one another, and the blood of Jesus his Son cleanses us from all sin. If we say we have no sin,

we deceive ourselves, and the truth is not in us.
(1 John 1:5–8)

It is not easy to confront a friend who is a brother or sister in Christ. I have lost friendships, and relationships have been broken because of this issue.

I remember riding in the car with my sister, Rachel, one day. We were discussing the issue I was having with the church. I shared with her how I had confronted Ryan about his lifestyle. Immediately, she quoted, "Judge not, that you be not judged" (Matt. 7:1). Wow! I was impressed. I went on to explain I wasn't judging a lost person but one who claimed to know the love of God and Christ as his savior. "It doesn't matter," she responded and then went on to ask me a question. "If I'm out shopping and I see my neighbor making out with someone other than his wife, are you saying that I'm supposed to confront him?"

"If he claims to be a Christian and a follower of Christ," I said. "Yes, it's your responsibility to go to him in love." I then gave her an example: If I see Sandy, who is a good friend and a sister in Christ, coming out a bar on Saturday night drunk, using the Lord's name in vain, and being hostile, it is my duty as a believer and a follower of Christ to confront her.

"Brothers, if anyone is caught in any transgression, you who are spiritual should restore him in a spirit of gentleness. Keep watch on yourself, lest you too be tempted" (Gal. 6:1).

We are not to overlook wrong behavior in the church, and that's what was happening where I attended. People in leadership were living contrary to God's Word and moral standards. Sound doctrine and a transformed life are essential in a Christian life and service.

I was obedient and my task was finished, and was I glad. But my task wasn't finished and only a starting point. God had a different plan. Homosexuality was not the only corruption in the church. I knew some of the leaders in the church were not walking in obedience. Their lifestyle was offensive to me and also to the God they proclaimed to know. Christ should be evident in our lives, especially when we are leaders in the church. How do we go out into the world and preach the gospel of Jesus Christ when we see evidence of active sin within our own church body (even those who have been appointed to be in leadership within the church)? My heart was broken. I sought godly counsel and prayed about the issue of having to confront the pastor whom I love.

How can one who claims to be a Christian be okay with homosexuality? In society, it is no longer seen as sin but rather a sexual identity and an alternative lifestyle. How does one who claims to be a Christian go to a bar every Saturday night, get drunk, and use the Lord's name in vain and then go to church Sunday morning? Does that make everything okay? We now fit into the world's standards instead of those set by the Lord.

I knew someone who committed adultery quite often. She was a friend who claimed to be a Christian. She attended church on a regular basis. When I confronted her, she claimed loudly, "We all fall under grace. Therefore, all is forgiven." The scripture that ran through my mind and I shared with her was:

> What then? Are we to sin because we are not under law but under grace? By no means! Do you not know that if you present yourselves to anyone as obedient slaves, you are slaves of the one whom you obey, either of sin, which leads to death, or of obedience, which leads to righteousness? (Rom. 6:15–16)

I still see my friend now and then, but the relationship has changed. I must insert here that I don't claim to have it all mastered. I identify with the Apostle Paul in his letter to Timothy.

> I thank him who has given me strength, Christ Jesus our Lord, because he judged me faithful, appointing me to his service, though formerly I was a blasphemer, persecutor, and insolent opponent. But I received mercy because I had acted ignorantly in unbelief, and the grace of our Lord

overflowed for me with the faith and love that are
in Christ Jesus. (1 Tim. 1:12–14)

We all struggle with some sin. It's what we do with it that matters. Many times, I've been on my knees at two in the morning, asking God's forgiveness and guidance. I don't sleep well when my soul is restless.

I had been praying for my church for some time now and even found myself dreading Sunday mornings. To be honest, I wanted to just walk away, but God had a different plan. This time, it didn't have anything to do with making chicken noodle soup, zucchini bread, or strawberry jam.

Each morning, I ask God to guide my steps and help me be a blessing to those whose paths I cross and salt and light to this dark world. Well, God guided me down a path I didn't want to pursue. Now it seemed He was asking me not to just quietly leave this fellowship but call into question what was going on in the church body. Ouch! I guess now it was time to put action to the prayer of my heart: "God, I love you. I want to please you and obey you."

"If you love me, you will keep my commandments" (John 14:15). This is the deepest desire of my heart.

God, being the sovereign, awesome God He is, had already been working in the hearts of the pastor and some of the leaders within the church. The pastor had begun preaching on the first epistle of Paul to the Corinthians, a letter in which Paul addressed problems that had developed in the church at Corinth. Then the Sunday came when it was time to preach First Corinthians 5:1a: "It is actually reported that there is sexual immorality among you…" My prayer was that it would not fall on deaf ears but on receptive hearts. When the pastor was finished with First Corinthians chapter 5, he himself admitted he was wrong for not holding his serving leaders accountable. Then he gave everyone in attendance a handout, which contained scripture:

Therefore be imitators of God, as beloved children. And walk in love, as Christ loved us and gave himself up for us, a fragrant offering and sacrifice to God. But sexual immorality and all impurity or covetousness must not even be named among you, as is proper among saints. Let there be no filthiness nor foolish talk nor crude joking, which are out of place, but instead let there be thanksgiving. For you may be sure of this, that everyone who is sexually immoral or impure, or who is covetous (that is, an idolater), has no inheritance in the kingdom of Christ and God. Let no one deceive you with empty words, for because of these things the wrath of God comes upon the sons of disobedience. Therefore do not become partners with them; for at one time you were darkness, but now you are light in the Lord. Walk as children of light (for the fruit of light is found in all that is good and right and true), and try to discern what is pleasing to the Lord. Take no part in the unfruitful works of darkness, but instead expose them. For it is shameful even to speak of the things that they do in secret. But when anything is exposed by the light, it becomes visible, for anything that becomes visible is light. Therefore it says Awake, O sleeper, and arise from the dead, and Christ will shine on you. Look carefully then how you walk, not as unwise but as wise, making the best use of the time, because the days are evil. Therefore do not be foolish, but understand what the will of the Lord is. And do not get drunk with wine, for that is debauchery, but be filled with the Spirit. (Eph. 5:1–18)

But I say, walk by the Spirit, and you will not gratify the desires of the flesh. For the desires of the flesh are against the Spirit, and the desires of the Spirit are against the flesh, for these are opposed to each other, to keep you from doing the things you want to do. But if you are led by the Spirit, you are not under the law. Now the works of the flesh are evident: sexual immorality, impurity, sensuality, idolatry, sorcery, enmity, strife, jealousy, fits of anger, rivalries, dissensions, divisions, envy, drunkenness, orgies, and things like these. I warn you, as I warned you before, that those who do such things will not inherit the kingdom of God. But the fruit of the Spirit is love, joy, peace, patience, kindness, goodness, faithfulness, gentleness, self-control; against such things there is no law. And those who belong to Christ Jesus have crucified the flesh with its passions and desires. If we live by the Spirit, let us also keep in step with the Spirit. Let us not become conceited, provoking one another, envying one another. (Gal. 5:16–26)

I believe we had a true revival in our church that day. Some left, but many repented and dedicated their lives to the Lord. When I walked into church the next Sunday, I could sense the presence of God—an awareness that had been absent for some time.

At the end of the day, when I lay my head on the pillow, I am at peace. God is in control when we find ourselves in the center of His will. My desire is on that day when I see Christ face to face, He will say, "Well done, my good and faithful servant."

Is God enough for such a time as this?

Chapter 12
Being Labeled

But now the righteousness of God has been manifested apart from the law, although the Law and the Prophets bear witness to it—the righteousness of God through faith in Jesus Christ for all who believe. For there is no distinction.

—Romans 3:21–22

During our senior year in high school, there was a yearbook we all got toward the end of the year. We had as many classmates sign it as we could. Some wrote long messages. Others simply said, "Great going to school with you. Good luck in the future." The ones who wrote few words or just signed their name knew nothing about me. There were a few friends who wrote a kind, friendly, fun, and compassionate note. These classmates were not the ones I went to class with. They were the ones on the varsity softball field and basketball court. They were the ones who knew me. They were the ones I never felt out of place with, as I did in several areas of my life. When on the softball or basketball team, you are just that—a team. If you are good, they really like you. I made that my purpose to be "good." It was not pride that was my driving force but acceptance and belonging. That statement "no man is an island" is very true. We all have a deep desire within us to be needed and accepted, valued and loved. At the end of the senior year, we also voted on different classmates and how we perceived them. Some of the labels were "Most Likely to Succeed," "Best Personality," "Most Athletic," "Class Clown," "Most Talkative," "Life of the Party," and "Class Flirt."

As we enter the adult world, we still have labels and tabs that identify us—who we are and what we are: CEO of a company, supervisor, soccer mom, super dad, chief of police, housewife, janitor, or musician just to name a few. There is nothing wrong with these identifying labels as long as they address more specifically who we are. What has happened within the church is something far more bothersome and frustrating. Labeling has continued within the church. We categorize sin as being big or little. This may sound far-fetched or even exaggerated, but it does exist within the body of Christ. Some of those little, not-so-bad sins like lying, pride, anger, and worry are just overlooked. Adultery, murder, idolatry, homosexuality, and divorce fall into the big sin category. It seems some of us have been labeled with our forgiven sin such as ex-adulterer, ex-murderer, ex-idolater, ex-homosexual, and ex-divorcee. What comes with these labels is a different standard and a greater acknowledgement for confession in order to be forgiven.

I confessed and repented of my sins, asking Jesus to come into my heart. I have found love, grace, mercy, and forgiveness with God the Father and Jesus Christ our Lord. Evidently, some churches have a different requirement. God's heavenly kingdom has accepted me, but many of those within the church are unable to accept God has wiped away all sin and cleansed my life, which has led to the transformation of my daily walk. This is happening mostly because we have a tendency to categorize sin and label people accordingly. Now, according to some, I am not only a sinner saved by grace but also labeled ex-homosexual rather than forgiven. "As far as the east is from the west, so far does He remove our transgressions from us" (Ps. 103:12). This scripture states I am no longer held guilty of any past sin.

I recently had the opportunity to go on a trip to Pennsylvania with my friend, Barb, and the seniors of her church. I had previously shared my testimony at a ladies' meeting at this church, so several of them knew who I was. When Barb had shared I was going and she was sharing a room with me, she was met with these words: "You are going to stay in the same room with Margaret?" Mind you, this was from a Christian. This is not an isolated incident. I know several who have shared their life story and how the love, grace, and mercy of God changed their life, only to find rejection and condemnation within the circle of believers.

My dear pastor, Dan Cummings, presented a sermon where he asked, "How many of you would have committed a sin last evening and come to a church wearing the sandwich sign on your back 'I committed adultery and so forth last evening'?" The church stands guilty because they lack the forgiveness and compassion God has granted on all people's behalf, but the human side of people refuses to forgive as Christ has forgiven them, Jesus Christ being our example.

When Pastor Cummings came to our church, everyone, myself included, wondered what he would be like. We all had our own ideas, likes, and dislikes; our view of how a preacher should preach. Is he going to teach the Word and challenge us or just keep reminding us God loves us and reaffirming that if we believe, everything will be okay? One of the first Sundays he was there, I remember walking into the service and seeing a huge rugged cross standing smack-dab in the center of the platform. *This is interesting*, I thought. In order to see anything, the choir, special music presenters, or the pastor had to look around, over, under, and many times through *the cross*. During the entire service, we had to deal with *that cross*. The pastor then preached that old familiar passage in John chapter 8.

> The scribes and the Pharisees brought a woman who had been caught in adultery, and placing her in the midst they said to him, "Teacher, this woman has been caught in the act of adultery. Now in the Law, Moses commanded us to stone such women. So what do you say?" This they said to test him, that they might have some charge to bring against him. Jesus bent down and wrote with his finger on the ground. And as they continued to ask him, he stood up and said to them, "Let him who is without sin among you be the first to throw a stone at her." And once more he bent down and wrote on the ground. But when they heard it, they

went away one by one, beginning with the older
ones, and Jesus was left alone with the woman
standing before him. Jesus stood up and said to
her, "Woman, where are they? Has no one condemned you?" She said, "No one, Lord." And
Jesus said, "Neither do I condemn you; go, and
from now on sin no more." (John 8:3–11)

After quoting Romans 3:23 ("For all have sinned and fall short
of the glory of God"), Pastor Dan then asked, "Is there any sin not
covered by the death of Jesus on the cross? Is there any sin he did
not die for?" Throughout the room, stones had been scattered, rep-
resenting various sins. Next, he invited any who would be willing to
lay their stone at the foot of the cross and confess their sin. I watched
in amazement as person after person approached the cross, laid their
stone at the foot, then went to the platform and publicly admitted
and confessed their sin. Everything from adultery to pride was confessed. We all stood together at the foot of the cross, standing equally
guilty and equally forgiven and covered by the blood of Jesus Christ.
When we label people, it is more often than not hurtful, degrading,
and destructive. We would expect this from the world, but we, as
believers in Jesus Christ, are not of this world.

I appeal to you therefore, brothers, by the mercies of God, to present your bodies as a living
sacrifice, holy and acceptable to God, which is
your spiritual worship. Do not be conformed to
this world, but be transformed by the renewal of
your mind, that by testing you may discern what
is the will of God, what is good and acceptable
and perfect. (Rom. 12:1–2)

Labels also cause division, destruction, and separation. And an
effect of these judgments, which are not according to God's instruction, much separation will be evident within the body of believers.
Jesus, speaking to the scribes, said, "If a kingdom is divided against

itself, that kingdom cannot stand. And if a house is divided against itself, that house will not be able to stand" (Mark 3:24–25). When we belong to God, we are his beloved children, joint heirs with Jesus and called to be saints. We are all sinners saved by grace. That is the only label that matters.

> I appeal to you, brothers, by the name of our Lord Jesus Christ, that all of you agree, and that there be no divisions among you, but that you be united in the same mind and the same judgment. (1 Cor. 1:10)
>
> Put on then, as God's chosen ones, holy and beloved, compassionate hearts, kindness, humility, meekness, and patience, bearing with one another and, if one has a complaint against another, forgiving each other; as the Lord has forgiven you, so you also must forgive. And above all these put on love, which binds everything together in perfect harmony. (Col. 3:12–14)
>
> Finally, all of you, have unity of mind, sympathy, brotherly love, a tender heart, and a humble mind. (1 Pet. 3:8)
>
> Behold, how good and pleasant it is when brothers dwell in unity! (Ps. 133:1)

Here is "Before the Throne of God Above," a hymn by Charitie Lees Smith:

> Before the throne of God above
> I have a strong, a perfect plea,
> A great High Priest whose name is Love
> Whoever lives and pleads for me.
> My name is graven on His hands,
> My name is written on His heart.
> I know that while in heaven He stands
> No tongue can bid me thence depart

When Satan tempts me to despair
And tells me of the guilt within,
Upward I look and see Him there
Who made an end to all my sin.
Because the sinless Savior died
My sinful soul is counted free,
For God the just is satisfied
To look on Him and pardon me.

Is God enough for such a time as this?

Chapter 13
Sharing the Gospel

> You are the light of the world. A city set on a hill cannot be hidden. Nor do people light a lamp and put it under a basket but on a stand, and it gives light to all in the house. In the same way, let your light shine before others, so that they may see your good works and give glory to your Father who is in heaven.
>
> —Matthew 5:14–16

Life seems to be a roller coaster of emotions. With each mountaintop experience, it seems you can always count on hitting the valley again soon. Happiness and joy can quickly turn into sadness and misery with just one phone call or a knock at the door. I am a people person. Whenever something exciting in my life happens, I want to share it with people I love and care about. I recently had the opportunity to visit the Creation Museum and the Ark Encounter in Kentucky. They were both eye-opening experiences. What made it more special was sharing the experience with people I love—Lois, Jeannie, and Barb. After returning home, I wanted to share the experience with other friends who knew we were going. After telling my friend, Kaye, she looked at me and said, "You're glowing." I've read about creation and Noah building the ark many times in the Scripture, I've also sat through many sermons on both subjects, but to visualize it seemed to make it more miraculous than previously experienced.

Many friends came to mind while I was walking through the museum, reliving creation from the beginning. I thought of Sandy,

Karen, and many of my SOLO friends who would share in my excitement. I thought of my friend, Carol, as I sat in the planetarium. I was awestruck as it pictured only a glimpse of the universe. It spoke of a vast number and size of galaxies, planets, stars, and the moon. I found myself speechless, unable to wrap my mind around what was so immense. How does one describe something so indescribable? One word: God! "In the beginning, God created the heavens and the earth" (Gen. 1:1). The Creation Museum, Ark Encounter, and planetarium were all pretty amazing. They carry with them the excitement, which is the power of God.

When watching the Olympics, World Series, Rose Bowl, Super Bowl, and Stanley Cup, everyone shares in their victory or defeat. It is always more fun and exciting when we share this with our friends. As believers, we have something much more wonderful than winning the gold medal or raising the Stanley Cup. As phenomenal as these moments are, and quite an achievement for sure, their victory and excitement only lasts for a moment compared to the powerful display of God, which is evident and eternal.

I have a deep desire within me to share the joy and peace I have in my heart since coming to know Jesus as my personal savior. This is a joy that will last for eternity. I want so badly to share with all my friends, family, and people whom God has brought into my life this story of love, grace, mercy, and truth. I also have a desire to have them sit with me at the table of the Marriage Supper of the Lamb.

> Then I heard what seemed to be the voice of a great multitude, like the roar of many waters and like the sound of mighty peals of thunder, crying out, Hallelujah! For the Lord our God the Almighty reigns. Let us rejoice and exult and give him the glory, for the marriage of the Lamb has come, and his Bride has made herself ready. (Rev. 19:6–7)

I have often thought how wonderful it would be to be a missionary. I know several. I love hearing their testimonies of what God has done in and through them. I remember Jessie telling a story of her Uncle Bill Rice who was a missionary. She would share how her Uncle Bill was intrigued by the Pigmy. God provided him the opportunity to visit a Pigmy village. Pigmy people are unusually short. The average height of an adult male is four feet and eleven inches. Bill Rice was well over six feet tall with white hair. The people of the village thought he was God. They wanted to build him a house so he would stay and live with them. Of course, Bill told them he was not God, but God had sent him to their village to tell them about the one true God and His gospel. The people of the village took Bill and introduced him to a certain old man in the village. This man would sleep during the day. Every night, he would climb a tree to the very top and gaze into the sky. He told Bill he did this because he believed there was a God out there somewhere so he looked at the stars, waiting and wondering. What a great portrait of Romans 1:19–20.

> For what can be known about God is plain to them, because God has shown it to them. For his invisible attributes, namely, his eternal power and divine nature, have been clearly perceived, ever since the creation of the world, in the things that have been made. So they are without excuse.

Bill told the man in the tree indeed there was a God, and that God had a message for him. He went on to share the message: the gospel of Jesus Christ. I love that story. How great is God! He loved that old man in a tree so much He sent someone halfway around the world to answer the question in the man's heart and soul. I'm sure the man in the village no longer had to climb a tree searching for God. The God he was looking for in the stars and the night sky now lives in his heart.

> "Praise the Lord, all nations! Extol Him all peoples! For great is His steadfast love toward us, and the faithfulness of the Lord endures forever. Praise the Lord!" (Ps. 117)

"For by grace you have been saved through
faith. And this is not your own doing; it is a gift
of God" (Eph. 2:8).

When we, God's people, are bonded together with God's mercy,
grace, love, and truth, not only do we have a deep, burning desire to
share that joy; we are also commanded by God to do so. "Declare
His glory among the nations, His marvelous works among all the
peoples! For great is the Lord, and greatly to be praised; He is to be
feared above all gods" (Pss. 96:3–4). We are not to be silent. When
we pray and ask God for opportunities to share His truth and what
He has done in our lives, we must always be ready, recognizing that
moment. Trust me, the opportunity could come when least expected.

One fall morning, I had stopped to visit my friend, Carol, at
her place of business, as I often did, just to say hi. We chatted for
a few minutes, then she walked me to my car, asking the common
question: "So what's on your agenda today?" I told her I was going
home to work on an outline. I thought the conversation would end,
we would give each other a hug, and I'd be on my way, but God had
a different plan. Carol asked, "An outline for what?"

I replied, "A church in Rochester had asked me to share my
testimony with their ladies." We then talked about what a testimony
is about. That being, how God has transformed my life. Not wanting
to share my testimony at the time and ending my comments there, I
was anxious to get into my car and exit.

Then her next words were, "And so?"

I knew exactly what those words were asking. Up until that
point in my walk with the Lord, I had only shared this one-on-one
freely and openly with three other people. Yes, I had shared my testimony in church and women's meetings several times, but I always
find it more difficult to share independently. I have lost several
friends along the way, and that always hurts and leaves a scar. I had
only been friends with Carol a short time, and to be honest, I wasn't
sure about her reaction. Was I willing to risk that friendship? I guess
the bigger question is was I willing to be obedient and trust God? I
was reluctant, even questioning God: "Now? Are you kidding me?" I

then shared with her how God had delivered me from a homosexual life, forgave my sin, and made me whole. I think it took all of two minutes, although it seemed like an eternity.

"Wow, that's pretty amazing!" she said. There was no sense of distance or discomfort. We then talked about God and who He is. Remember, I was getting in my car, ready to leave, before this took place. As I left, she hugged me, saying, "All is good." Reassuring and comforting words, for sure, and yes, we are still good friends. I had no intention of telling Carol of my past. I saw no reason for it. Evidently, God had a reason. I know God is most pleased when He is glorified by my obedience, and I don't miss an opportunity to share my story. When I got home, I thanked God for the opportunity, boldness, and ability to share the truth—His truth.

My pastor, Tim, recently shared an experience he had while attending Bible college. One of their assignments was a trip to New York to street preach. This was in the early nineties, much more common and accepted at that time. They were talking with people in the street and handing out gospel tracts. The title of the tract they were handing out was "Where will you go when you die?" While Tim was reading the tract, he was approached by a man who asked him, "Is this something for me?"

"Absolutely," Tim responded. He then shared the information on the tract and the gospel of Jesus Christ with the man. That day, that man confessed his sins and accepted Jesus Christ as his savior. There was rejoicing in heaven.

Jesus, after sharing the parable of the lost sheep and how one rejoices when it is found, concluded the parable by saying, "Just so, I tell you, there will be more joy in heaven over one sinner who repents than over ninety-nine righteous persons who need no repentance" (Luke 15:7).

Before the man left that afternoon, he told Tim he was gay, and he just came from the doctor's office and was diagnosed with AIDS. Bitterness and anger began to build inside Tim's heart. Unlike the rejoicing in heaven, Tim could not rejoice in this situation because of his feelings toward those who are caught in the sin of homosexuality. Why couldn't he rejoice? Because that man wasn't just a liar, thief, adulterer, drunkard, idolater, or greedy; he was a homosexual. Tim wrestled all night. Some would say he had a guilty conscience. To a believer, it's much more than a guilty conscience; it's being chastened and disciplined by our heavenly Father. "My son, do not despise the Lord's discipline or be weary of his reproof, for the Lord reproves him who he loves" (Prov. 3:11–12)

When Christ died on the cross, He died for all sin. Yes, even the homosexual. "Christ died for our sins in accordance with the Scriptures, that he was buried, that he was raised on the third day in accordance with the Scriptures" (1 Cor. 15:3b–4). When God's children make wrong choices, God chastens us to keep us safe and bring us back to holiness.

There was a dark cloud hanging over Tim that night, and he knew it. He confessed the bitterness, anger, and rebellion in his heart because of his own prejudice. Through this obedience, God was true to His word and forgave him. "If we confess our sins, he is faithful and just to forgive us our sins and to cleanse us from all unrighteousness" (1 John 1:9).

The experience Tim had in leading the homosexual man to Christ was shared on a local Christian radio program, and the man Tim had dealt with called the radio station saying he was the individual they were talking about. The radio station was then able to talk to him and connect him with a local church. God doesn't leave us on our own nor does he do things halfway. God also doesn't waste anything. "And we know that for those who love God all things work together for good, for those who are called according to His purpose" (Rom. 8:28).

Just this past year, Tim would learn his own son was gay. The encounter Tim had with the gay man several years ago would not only prove to be helpful but also encouraging. Had that situation not have happened, Tim's anger, bitterness, and hate would have been directed at his own son. Tim knows and understands God's love, grace, mercy, and forgiveness is extended unto all who call on His name, even the homosexual. "For there is no distinction between Jew and Greek; the same Lord is Lord of all, bestowing His riches on all who call on Him. For everyone who calls on the name of the Lord shall be saved" (Rom. 10:12–13).

One of my most cherished passages in the Scripture is the story of Jesus and the sinful woman who wiped His feet with her tears.

> One of the Pharisees asked him to eat with him, and he went into the Pharisee's house and reclined at table. And behold, a woman of the city, who was a sinner, when she learned that he was reclining at table in the Pharisee's house, brought an alabaster flask of ointment, and standing behind him at his feet, weeping, she began to wet his feet with her tears and wiped them with the hair of her head and kissed his feet and anointed them with the ointment. Now when the Pharisee who had invited him saw this, he said to himself, "If this man were a prophet, he would have known who and what sort of woman this is who is touching him, for she is a sinner." And Jesus answering said to him, "Simon, I have something to say to you." And he answered, "Say it, Teacher." "A certain moneylender had two debtors. One owed five hundred denarii, and the other fifty. When they could not pay, he cancelled the debt of both. Now which of them will love him more?" Simon answered, "The one, I suppose, for whom he cancelled the larger debt." And he said to him, "You have judged rightly." Then turning toward the woman he said to Simon, "Do you see this woman? I entered your house; you gave me no water for my feet, but she has wet my feet with her tears and wiped them with her hair. You gave me no kiss, but from the time I came in she has not ceased to kiss my feet. You did not anoint my head with oil, but she has anointed my feet with ointment. Therefore I tell you, her sins, which are many, are forgiven—for she loved much. But

he who is forgiven little, loves little." And he said
to her, "Your sins are forgiven." (Luke 7:36–48)

There are several points in this story that are interesting. The
Pharisees were a religious group who held themselves in high esteem.
They were righteous men above the common people and, therefore,
separated themselves from others. There was no way that woman of
the city would be welcomed in such a setting, yet she had her mind
and heart set on one person: Jesus. She never spoke a word; she didn't
have to. Jesus knew her heart. Her expression of love and adoration
to Jesus was more than obvious.

Sadly, many churches have the mindset of the Pharisees. They
are not only good people but also righteous and keepers of the law.
But Jesus himself called them hypocrites. He saw past their outward
appearance with their flowing robes and tassels, seeking approval
for themselves. Many people judge a person by the clothes they
wear, the car they drive, or the house where they live. Ultimately, it
is the heart that matters. "For the Lord sees not as man sees: man
looks on the outward appearance, but the Lord looks on the heart"
(1 Sam. 16:7b).

God is in the business of transforming the hearts of men. He does
that by calling man to himself and by his people communicating God's
love for them. Jesus, when praying to His Father in heaven, said:

> As you sent me into the world, so I have sent
> them into the world. And for their sake I con-
> secrate myself, that they may also be sanctified
> in truth. I do not ask for these only, but also for
> those who will believe in me through their word,
> that they may all be one, just as you, Father, are
> in me, and I in you, that they also may be in
> us, so that the world may believe that you have
> sent me. The glory that you have given me I have
> given to them, that they may be one even as we
> are one. (John 17:18–22)

I love hearing people's testimonies and what God has done in their lives. What's even more exciting is if I knew that person before they came to know Christ as their personal savior, then it's not just a story being told but the real thing. Seeing truly is believing. I've heard several people say they don't have an exciting testimony. They never experienced drugs, had an abortion, were an alcoholic or even a homosexual. It doesn't matter what we came from or who we were. We, as believers, have first-hand experience in the understanding of God's forgiveness, grace, mercy, and love. We are now a child of the King, and He reigns in our hearts.

My desire is to share this good news with everyone I know. I want them to experience the same peace and joy that lives within my heart. The best way to do this, I believe, is to develop a relationship and friendship with the individual. Get to know them and earn their trust. Meet them on neutral ground. Many times, I find people who have just met someone, and right off the bat, they invite them to church. I'm not saying that's a bad thing, but to be honest, church can be intimidating, scary, and often unfriendly. I find I get to know someone better by having lunch together or just having a cup of coffee and a piece of pie. Remember the parable of the Good Samaritan.

> And behold, a lawyer stood up to put him to the test, saying, "Teacher, what shall I do to inherit eternal life?" He said to him, "What is written in the Law? How do you read it?" And he answered, "You shall love the Lord your God with all your heart and with all your soul and with all your strength, and with all your mind, and your neighbor as yourself." And he said to him, "You have answered correctly; do this, and you will live." But he, desiring to justify himself, said to Jesus, "And who is my neighbor?" Jesus replied, "A man was going down from Jerusalem to Jericho, and he fell among robbers, who stripped him and beat him and departed, leaving him half dead. Now by chance a priest was going down that road, and

when he saw him he passed by on the other side. So likewise a Levite, when he came to the place and saw him, passed by on the other side. But a Samaritan, as he journeyed, came to where he was, and when he saw him, he had compassion. He went to him and bound up his wounds, pouring on oil and wine. Then he sat him on his own animal and brought him to an inn and took care of him. And the next day he took out two denarii and gave them to the innkeeper saying, 'Take care of him, and whatever more you spend, I will repay you when I come back.' Which of these three, do you think, proved to be a neighbor to the man who fell among the robbers?" He said, "The one who showed him mercy." And Jesus said to him, "You go and do likewise." (Luke 10:25–37)

This parable answers the question: who is my neighbor? We shouldn't confine our love and compassion for our neighbor based on condition. Nationality, job, appearance, or convenience should not prevent or hinder our willingness to love our neighbor as our self, no matter who they are or where they come from. The world we now live in is getting darker every day and full of lies, hate, and no moral standards. Even in our churches, truth is watered down, and sin is not talked about. The light that once shone bright seems to be getting dim and often completely blown out. People are looking for something different from the world. People are looking for hope. We know that hope is found in Christ alone. All Christians are to be examples of the light that was given to us through faith and believing in God. We, as believers, have a story to tell, and it's the greatest story ever told. The words to that familiar hymn, "I Love to Tell the Story" by Katherine Hankey and William G. Fischer, should be our desire.

I love to tell the story
Of unseen things above,
Of Jesus and His glory

Of Jesus and His love.
I love to tell the story,
Because I know 'tis true;
It satisfied my longings
As nothing else can do.
I love to tell the story;
'Tis pleasant to repeat
What seems each time I tell it,
More wonderfully sweet.
I love to tell the story;
For some have never heard
The message of salvation
From God's own holy Word.
I love to tell the story,
For those who knew it best
Seem hungering and thirsting
To hear it like the rest.
And when, in scenes of glory,
I sing a new, new song,
Twill be the old, old story,
That I have loved so long.
I love to tell the story!
'Twill be my theme in glory
To tell the old, old story
Of Jesus and His love.

Is God enough for such a time as this?

Chapter 14
God Our Father

And I will be a father to you, and you shall be sons
and daughters to me, says the Lord Almighty.
—2 Corinthians 6:18

It's Christmas—my most favorite time of the year. The Christmas trees, decorated homes and towns, and Christmas carols being sung are all things that make my heart a little happier and put a smile to my face. The excitement of little children waking up on Christmas morning to see the pretty packages under the tree, anxious to rip them apart. On my tree, I have a favorite ornament. It is a sheep holding a birthday cake in front of him with the words "Happy Birthday, Jesus." Behind his back, as if it were to be a surprise, is a little package with a tag that reads "To my Savior." I like to think in that package is my heart. I believe that would be the very best gift I could offer Jesus. The first and most precious gift, of course, was Jesus being given.

> And while they were there the time came for her to give birth. And she gave birth to her first born son and wrapped him in swaddling clothes and laid him in a manger, because there was no place for him in the inn. And in the same region there were shepherds out in the field, keeping watch over their flock by night. And an angel of the Lord appeared to them, and the glory of the Lord shone around them, and they were filled with

great fear. And the angel said to them, "Fear not for behold, I bring you good news of great joy that will be for all the people. For unto you is born this day in the city of David a Savior, who is Christ the Lord. And this will be a sign for you: you will find a baby wrapped in swaddling clothes and lying in a manger." And suddenly there was with the angel a multitude of heavenly hosts praising God and saying, "Glory to God in the highest, and on earth peace among those with whom he is pleased." (Luke 2:6–14)

Because of Jesus's birth, death, and resurrection, all who will believe in Him will no longer be separated from God.

But when the fullness of time had come, God sent forth his Son, born of a woman, born under the law, to redeem those who were under the law, so that we might receive adoption as sons. And because you are sons, God has sent the Spirit of his Son into our hearts, crying, "Abba! Father!" So you are no longer a slave, but a son, and if a son, then an heir through God. (Gal. 4:4–7)

We now have a heavenly Father who cares for us deeply and wants so much to be a part of our lives.

Recently, I was shopping at Home Depot. It was a Saturday, when they often have father-son projects. The store provides the supplies needed, and the fathers and their sons work together to build it. That day, they were creating their own race cars, complete with paint, decals, and numbers. The boys were between six and eight years old.

One little boy was totally into making his race car. He struggled trying to get the wheels to fit right as his father was busy on the phone. The dad was there in person but totally clueless as to what his son was trying to accomplish.

The second father and son were quite the opposite. The little boy watched as his father built that race car. The son tried desperately to be involved, but the father did things his way. The son wanted the car to be yellow, but the dad chose red. When the boy picked the number 8, the dad overruled him again and perfectly placed the number 3 on its doors and hood. The car was beautiful, but the car was the dad's car. The son had no involvement at all.

Then there was a father and son who caught my attention, and I smiled as I watched. The son was building the car as the father carefully watched. The only time the dad would help was when the son would ask how something fit together. The dad would also intervene when he saw his son doing something the wrong way. He would not only show him the correct way but also explain why it had to go the way it did. They were a team, and the car was theirs—a joint effort. When the car was complete, the little boy proudly held it while someone took their picture.

This is a wonderful picture of us and our heavenly Father. He wants so much to be a part of our lives in every aspect. The same God who is creator and sovereign over all things cares for you and me.

> For God is the King of all the earth; sing praises with a psalm! God reigns over the nations; God sits on his holy throne. The princes gather as the people of the God of Abraham. For the shields of the earth belong to God; He is highly exalted! (Pss. 47:7–9)
>
> The Lord reigns; He is robed in majesty; The Lord is robed; He has put on strength as his belt. Yes, the world is established; it shall never be moved. Your throne is established from of old; you are from everlasting. The floods have lifted up, O Lord, the floods have lifted up their voice; the floods lift up their roaring. Mightier than the thunders of many waters, mightier than the waves of the sea, the Lord on high is mighty! Your decrees are very trustworthy: holiness befits your house, O Lord, forevermore. (Ps. 93)

The God who reigns over the universe, the great I Am, is our heavenly Father.

George Beverly Shea wrote these words:

> There's the wonder of sunset at evening,
> The wonder of sunrise I see;
> But the wonder of wonder that thrills my soul
> Is the wonder that God loves me.

God is fully aware of our needs, and He is capable and willing to supply them. "And My God will supply every need of yours according to His riches in glory in Christ Jesus" (Phil. 4:19). As children of God, while here on earth, we daily experience His love, grace, mercy, power, wisdom, and gifts.

While camping with some friends this past summer, we were visiting with Scott and Jen. Scott is a pastor whom I've mentioned before. They have a great ministry, reaching out to teens and people in the community. It's called "Beulah Land Retreats." They also have a guest house they offer to people in ministry who just need to get away.

Jen was busy vacuuming their van, getting ready to take some ladies to a retreat out of town. I noticed the vacuum cleaner she was using not only looked brand new but also was one of those fancy, expensive vacuums. My curiosity got to me, so I said to her, "Wow, Jen. That's a pretty fancy vacuum you have."

She smiled and proceeded to tell me how it basically fell into her lap really cheap. If anyone else was telling me this story and the price she paid for it, I would not have believed them, but it was Jen, so I believed every word. She went on to share how God had supplied many other items for their ministry and made provisions in times of need. After both of us sharing with each other, she looked at me and said, "Isn't it great being one of God's kids?" Later that day, and ever since, I've tried to grasp what that statement means. Almighty God is my Father, and I am one of His kids!

I began to ask many of my friends how God has cared and provided for them. It is an interesting conversation, and many times, the exchange goes on and on and on and on. God is our protector and provider.

My friend LuAnn shared with me how an angel appeared out of nowhere to intervene and prevent what could have been a catastrophe. She was driving her Nash Rambler down Woodward Avenue with her four-year-old daughter and her friend standing in the back seat, looking out the window. The Nash Rambler was made in the early fifties, so seat belts were not common in most cars. LuAnn remembered pulling into a gas station on Woodward to get gas. She was walking into the station to pay for gas when she noticed her car rolling down the incline toward Woodward. Cars were zooming by, and the two little girls, standing in the back seat, were oblivious to what was about to happen. At that moment, LuAnn noticed a man who came from nowhere walking calmly toward her car. He put his hands on the car, stopped it from rolling into traffic, and proceeded to push the car back up to the pump. LuAnn jumped into the car to put it into park and anxiously got out to express her gratitude. When she jumped out her car, the man who had miraculously appeared just at the right place, at the right time, was nowhere to be seen. I'm sure LuAnn was in and out her car in five to ten seconds flat. An angel, maybe? A miracle, for sure. God's protection absolutely!

My friend Carol shared an unusual event that took place during her college years, many years ago. Carol was driving down the interstate on her way from University of Michigan when she had a flat tire. A young, attractive girl alone, stranded on the interstate in Detroit, is not a good situation in anybody's book. As she pulled off to the side of the road, a car pulled off right behind her. A man got out and said to her, "I noticed you have a flat tire. I'd like to help." Of course, there was no spare tire. The man put the tire in his trunk and told her to hop in as there was a tire repair shop just up the road. I can't imagine what was going through Carol's mind at the time. She did say she whispered a prayer as she got in the man's car. How many of us being in a time of desperation or uncertainty, remember to ask our heavenly Father for help? When we even silently pray to Him, "Help me," we are expressing our faith that God is sufficient, and we are completely dependent on Him.

"Casting all your anxieties on him, because He cares for you" (1 Pet. 5:7).

"And this is the confidence that we have toward Him, that if we ask anything according to His will He hears us" (1 John 5:14).

On their way to the tire shop, the man told Carol he was a born-again Christian. He got the tire fixed, paid for it, and went back to put it on her car. When she thanked him, he simply said he wanted to assist in any way he could before the wrong person came along. Was Carol just plain lucky that night? Not at all! She was being cared for by her heavenly Father who had heard and answered her whispered prayer.

My friend Barb was delayed in leaving her son's home one day. She was up north and needed to be home that afternoon for appointments, but God had a different plan. She was unable to leave because her car was blocked in by Jen's van, and Jen was still sleeping. Barb patiently waited for Jen to wake up, and when Jen moved her van, Barb was on her way. As Barb got onto I-75, she noticed it was backed up for miles. Ahead was a major accident with several cars involved. Immediately, Barb recognized she could have been involved had she left when she had planned. She said a thank-you prayer to her heavenly Father for His protection.

Several years ago, my friends and I were heading up north for a camping trip. We were traveling down I-75 on our motorcycles. Yes, I do own and drive a motorcycle and always with a helmet. I was in the lead, traveling about sixty-five miles per hour on the outside lane, when all of a sudden, I was thrown from my bike. At that, moment the only prayer I could muster was "Oh help." I saw I was rapidly headed straight for the guard rail and thought it was going to hurt. As I was rolling, bouncing off the pavement and heading toward a very solid guardrail, I remembered not being able to move any part of my body. It was as though I was being held. Something or someone had wrapped themselves around me, and I was being cushioned. I also landed just shy of the guardrail. When I think about it, I actually could have been killed, but all I suffered was severe scratches on my right arm. My bike didn't fare so well as it was totaled. It was a miracle and a great example of the benefits of having God as my heavenly Father.

This is the same God who parted the Red Sea to protect his children from Pharaoh and his army (Exod. 14). The same God who protected Daniel after being thrown into the lion's den by King Darius (Dan. 6). It is He who protects His children even today. "He who dwells in the shelter of the Most High will abide in the shadow of the Almighty. I will say to the Lord, 'My refuge and My fortress, My God in whom I trust'" (Pss. 91:1–2).

God is also our provider. My friends Sue and Ed shared with me one of several stories of how God intervenes and provides. Sue and Ed had their two children in Christian schools. When Ed got laid off work, they both realized they could no longer afford tuition. They went to the school to make arrangements to withdraw the two kids from the school and enroll them in public school. At that time, they were told tuition had been paid for both children for as long as Ed was laid off. It was around the same time when they returned to their car after church and found a dish towel on the front seat. Inside that towel was a wad of money. They never really knew who left the money or paid the tuition for their children. Knowing them, I'm sure they were grateful to God for His provision.

Our church has a food ministry. We pick up food from the food bank and distribute it to the community. Many times, we get fresh produce. Recently, after the truck was just loaded with tons of fresh tomatoes and produce, it broke down on the way back to the church. Of course, it was ten degrees outside, and naturally, everything froze. You know what happens to frozen tomatoes when they thaw? A mess! A slimy, juicy mess! To top it off, the boxes were inside our fellowship room at church. That was the only place we had to put everything. Ed had the task of cleanup. He is retired with all kinds of time, so they say. He is also the pastor's dad, so how could he refuse? Ed was not only covered with rotten tomatoes and juice squishing between his toes but also responsible for cooking pancakes, bacon, and sausage for the Bible study that evening. Needless to say, he was not in the greatest of moods.

We have different groups use our church for meetings. One of the men from a meeting met Ed in the parking lot and asked Ed what he was doing. I'm sure it was the tomatoes all over Ed that piqued an interest. After Ed told him the whole story and how the truck was in the repair shop, the man asked Ed how much it would cost to repair the truck. Ed told him about two thousand dollars and that we had about half of that raised. At that moment, the man pulled out his wallet and gave Ed the remaining thousand dollars to pay toward getting our truck fixed. A coincidence? No. A miracle? Yes! God does provide.

Two weeks before Christmas, I ended up in the hospital with pneumonia. When I got home, all I felt like eating was soup. My friends, who graciously took care of my dog until I got home, had dinner for me on the stove. The next day, I was searching my canned goods for a can of soup when one of my friends called and said she was stopping by with some clam chowder from a local restaurant. *Wow!* I thought. *That's much better than canned soup.* The next day, my friends at the flower shop I work for delivered some chicken noodle soup. *Okay, now I'm getting spoiled,* I thought. The next day, Lois came by with some yummy squash soup. The next day, my wonderful neighbor brought me individual servings of cream of broccoli soup and tomato along with a BLT. I didn't tell anyone I was hungry for soup. I had fresh soup every day and no duplicates. Now that truly is amazing. God cares about all our needs (and even some wants), great and small.

The same God who rained down bread from heaven to feed the Israelites in the wilderness (Exod. 16) is our provider today. The same God who fed the five thousand with just five loaves and two fished (Matt. 4) provides for His people today. These are but a few examples. I could share story after story of God's protection and provision for His people in biblical times and presently. From parting the Red Sea to a bowl of hot soup, God demonstrates His protection, provision, and love for His children. Yes, indeed, it's great being one of God's kids. The omnipresent, omnipotent God is our Father. He only wants what's best for His children.

For I know the plans I have for you declares the Lord, plans for welfare and not for evil, to give you a future and a hope. (Jer. 29:11)

But, as it is written, what no eye has seen, nor ear heard, nor the heart of man imagined, what God has prepared for those who love Him. (1 Cor. 2:9)

I am a child of the Most High God. Are you?
Is God enough for such a time as this?

"I Give You Freedom" (The Whippoorwill Song)
Al Smith

I set the boundaries of the ocean vast,
Carved out the mountains from the distant past,
Molded a man from the miry clay,
Breathed in him life, but he went astray.

I own the cattle on a thousand hills;
I write the music for the whippoorwills,
Control the planets with their rocks and rills,
But give you freedom to use your own will.

I hold the waters in my mighty hand,
Spread out the heavens with a single span,
Make all creation tremble at my voice,
But my own sons come to me by choice.

Even the oxen know the Masters stall,
And sheep will recognize the shepherd's call,
I could demand your love—I own you twice;
But only willing love is worth the price.

And if you want me to, I'll make you whole;
I'll only do it though if you say so.
I'll never force you, for I love you so;
I give you freedom—is it yes or no?

Before any of us can have salvation, or become a child of the Most High God, we must first realize we are sinners and, therefore, separated from God.

The Word of God tells us, "Because, if you confess with your mouth that Jesus is Lord and believe in your heart that God raised him from the dead, you will be saved" (Rom. 10:9).

Jesus is waiting for you. There is nothing a person needs to do or fix before we can come to Him. Come to Him just as you are, and He will not only forgive you but also give you a new heart!

Here is a suggested prayer:

> God, I realize I am separated from you because of sin in my life. I believe you sent your Son, Jesus Christ, to die on the cross that I might have eternal life. I confess I am a sinner. Please forgive my sins and cleanse me from all unrighteousness. I ask you to come into my heart today.

If you prayed this prayer or a similar prayer and meant it with all of your heart, God is faithful. "As far as the east is from the west, so far does he remove our transgressions from us" (Ps. 103:12).

Welcome to the family of God. I encourage you to find a local Bible-believing church and become involved.

Yes, my friend, God is enough for such a time as this!

About the Author

Margaret was brought up and still lives in Michigan. A retired letter carrier, she enjoys sports, camping, and being outdoors and around the water. Margaret loves animals and having her German shepherd, Roxy, by her side. Allie

She loves people and being a part of their lives. Serving them and her King is her heart's desire.